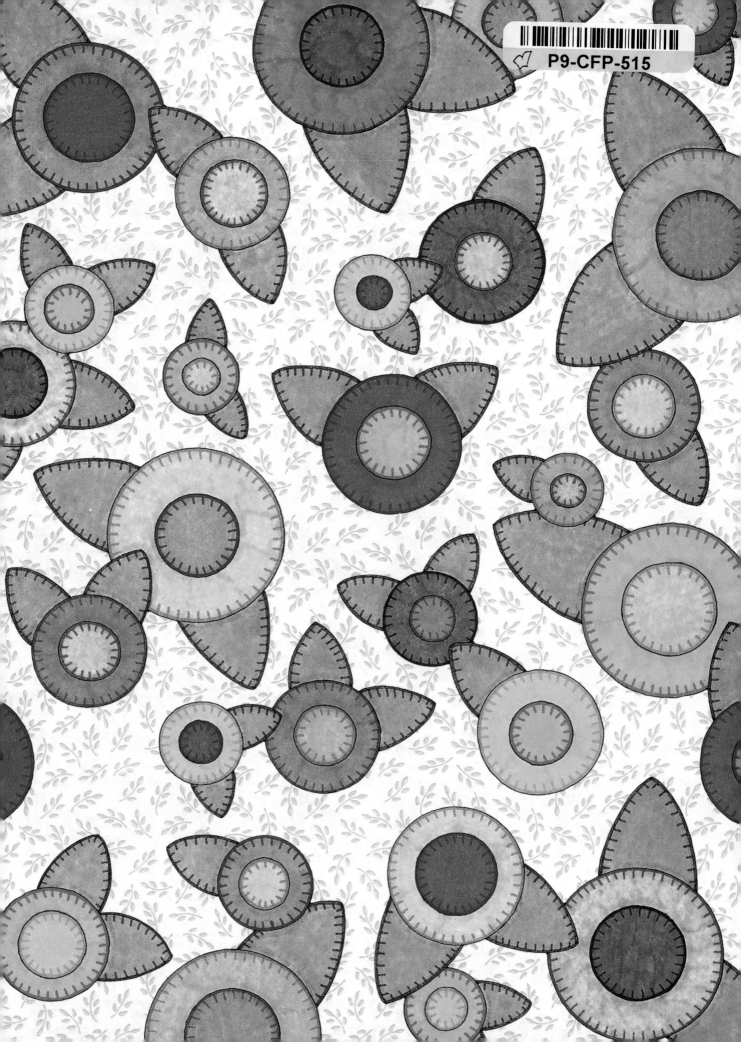

MARY ENGELBREIT

DECORATING IDEAS

PROJECTS TO MAKE for INDOORS AND OUT

Meredith® Press
Des Moines, Iowa

Meredith® Press
An imprint of Meredith® Books

Mary Engelbreit: Decorating Ideas—
Projects to Make for Indoors and Out
Editor: Carol Field Dahlstrom
Technical Editor: Susan M. Banker
Graphic Designer: Angela Haupert Hoogensen
Copy Chief: Catherine Hamrick
Copy and Production Editor: Terri Fredrickson
Contributing Copy Editor: Judith Stern Friedman
Contributing Proofreaders: Diane Doro, Gretchen
    Kauffman, Arianna McKinney
Photographers: Andy Lyons Cameraworks,
    Scott Little
Technical Illustrator: Chris Neubauer Graphics
Electronic Production Coordinator: Paula Forest
Editorial and Design Assistants: Judy Bailey,
    Mary Lee Gavin, Karen Schirm
Book Production Managers: Pam Kvitne,
    Marjorie J. Schenkelberg

Meredith® Books
Editor in Chief: James D. Blume
Design Director: Matt Strelecki
Managing Editor: Gregory H. Kayko

Director, Retail Sales and Marketing:
    Terry Unsworth
Director, Sales, Special Markets: Rita McMullen
Director, Sales, Premiums: Michael A. Peterson
Director, Sales, Retail: Tom Wierzbicki
Director, Book Marketing: Brad Elmitt
Director, Operations: George A. Susral
Director, Production: Douglas M. Johnston

Vice President, General Manager:
    Jamie L. Martin

Meredith Publishing Group
President, Publishing Group:
    Stephen M. Lacy
Vice President, Finance & Administration:
    Max Runciman

Meredith Corporation
Chairman and Chief Executive Officer:
    William T. Kerr

Chairman of the Executive Committee:
    E. T. Meredith III

All of us at Meredith® Press are dedicated to
providing you with information and ideas to
create beautiful and useful projects. We welcome
your comments and suggestions. Write to us at:
Meredith® Press, Crafts Editorial Department,
1716 Locust St., Des Moines, IA 50309-3023.

If you would like to purchase any of our books,
check wherever quality books are sold. Visit our
website at bhg.com.

Cover Illustration: Mary Engelbreit Studios

the comforts of home

hen I'm at home, either in my house or in my garden, there is a sense of comfort I find nowhere else. Being at home simply feels good, and I treasure the times I spend there.

My home is a personal haven—a place where I can express my tastes, pamper myself, and celebrate with the special people who are dear to my heart. Whether I am in one of my rooms or in an area of the yard, I can enjoy being surrounded by the things I love to make and collect.

That's why I enjoy adding handmade touches throughout the house, porch, gardens, and walkways. They not only decorate the spaces, but they also entertain, amuse, and make a statement about who I am.

I know you like creating a warm and welcoming atmosphere at your home too. That's why I am sharing these delightful projects with you. From lively garden accessories (like the easy, colorful rock flowers on page 94) to cuddly keepsake quilts and pillows (see pages 34 and 62), you'll find many fun items to craft for your own indoor and outdoor living spaces.

Enjoy making your favorite projects from this book. I'm sure you'll find success with the step-by-step instructions and patterns to guide you along.

As always, here's wishing you happy crafting hours and many cherished times at home surrounded by the things you love.

Mary Engelbreit

contents

PAGE 10

1 gather 'round the table

Every get-together will turn into a memory-making event with these clever projects gracing the table and the hostess.

2 nighty-night

Escape to your own private retreat—a bedroom filled with fanciful pillows, comfy quilts, and dreamlike accessories.

3 sweet little rooms

Turn your favorite corner of the house into a special nook with these handmade touches adding personality plus.

4 special touches

From an heirloom-quality cross-stitch sampler to easy-to-make stenciled lampshades, this chapter is filled with fun accent projects.

PAGE 62

PAGE 160

PAGE 168

prettied-up porches & patios 5

Spread some whimsy outside by making bright and cheerful embellishments that say "welcome" to one and all.

come to the garden 6

These clever outdoor accents will bloom long after the last petal falls from your growing beauties.

for our nature friends 7

Show your love of nature by crafting special projects for your favorite wildlife pals and family pets.

outdoor entertaining 8

Whether you want to set the table using sweet name cards or decorate with glistening sparklers, you're sure to find just the right project for your next gathering.

inspiration
is all around

When Mary Engelbreit sits down to put her artistic renderings on paper, she doesn't have to look far for inspiration. Mary may get an idea by gazing through her studio window watching a little bird splash about in a puddle of fresh rainwater. Or she may want to capture a special moment shared with a close friend or member of the family.

CHAPTER 1
GATHER 'ROUND THE TABLE

CHAPTER 2
NIGHTY-NIGHT

CHAPTER 3
SWEET LITTLE ROOMS

Mary Engelbreit uses the world around her and life's rewards as her inspiration. She captures the magic of it all in her wonderful greeting card art. For more than four decades, she has been sharing this magic with millions of fans and collectors of her classic illustrations.

CHAPTER 4
SPECIAL TOUCHES

CHAPTER 5
PRETTIED-UP
PORCHES &
PATIOS

In this fun, show-you-how book, you'll discover wonderful projects you can make—each inspired by one of Mary's enchanting scenes. Use these warm and whimsical creations to decorate the inside of your home as well as your outdoor spaces, helping you express your personal style and creativity.

CHAPTER 6
COME TO THE GARDEN

CHAPTER 7
FOR OUR NATURE FRIENDS

CHAPTER 8
OUTDOOR ENTERTAINING

As you dream through the book and choose your favorite projects, study Mary's greeting cards along the way. You'll discover wonderful motifs and patterns that will bring a smile to your face and cheer to your heart.

Enjoy this collection of step-by-step projects as well as the art that inspired them. The next time you are awed by nature or blessed with a treasured moment, look to the experience as inspiration for expressing your own talents in and around your home.

gather 'round the table

Some of the best times spent with family and friends are when we prepare for meals and enjoy each other's company as we gather 'round the table. These creative projects make every get-together a time of celebration.

floral napkin rings

Make every gathering special with these clay creations. The easy-to-form clay is shaped, baked, and then glued to a purchased napkin ring.

WHAT YOU'LL NEED

Wood napkin rings
Acrylic paints in yellow, black, and white
Small and fine liner paintbrushes
Bakeable clay, such as Sculpey, in pink, white, lavender, baby blue, green, red, and yellow
Small sharp knife
Glass baking dish
Thick white crafts glue
Clear gloss spray varnish

HERE'S HOW

1 Paint the napkin rings a solid color or paint them yellow with edges trimmed in black and white checks. To paint checks, first paint the rim area white. Let the paint dry. Using a fine liner paintbrush, paint black squares over the white paint. Let it dry.

2 Shape the flowers from clay. *To make round flowers,* roll a small ball about the size of a raisin and gently flatten it. Roll a smaller ball for the center and press it onto the larger piece. *To make blue and purple flowers,* roll small balls from blue or light purple clay. Arrange the balls in a circle and gently press them together. Roll a small white or dark purple ball for the center. Pinch five or six points as shown in the photograph, *right.* Roll a smaller yellow ball for the center. Gently press them together.

3 To make leaves, form small oval shapes from green clay. Make a crease down the center with a small sharp knife.

4 To make hearts, form a rounded triangle from pink clay. Shape the top to form a heart.

5 Place all clay shapes on a glass baking dish, leaving room around each piece. Bake the clay shapes in an oven according to the manufacturer's instructions. Remove from oven and let cool.

6 Glue the clay shapes onto the painted napkin rings as desired. Let the glue dry.

7 In a well-ventilated work area, spray the entire napkin ring with clear gloss varnish. Let it dry.

blooming tea cozy

Have a tea party at a moment's notice with this flower-laden cozy gracing your table. Tiny floral buttons add to the summery design.

WHAT YOU'LL NEED

Tracing paper and pencil
Scissors
½ yard blue-and-white checked fabric
Paperbacked fusible webbing
¼ yard white-on-white print fabric for flowers
3×10-inch piece of green fabric for leaves
3×6-inch piece of green print fabric for leaves
2×10-inch piece of yellow fabric for flower centers
Matching threads
Two 12×15-inch pieces of batting
Red embroidery floss; needle
1 yard of ½-inch-wide red flat trim
½ yard lining fabric
Seven ¾-inch red flower buttons

HERE'S HOW

(finished size 9¾×12 inches)

1 Enlarge and trace the tea cozy pattern, *page 14*, onto tracing paper. Use the pattern to trace two shapes on the blue-and-white checked fabric. On the front piece, trace the flower placement. Cut out the cozy front leaving approximately 1½ inches all around to allow for quilting.

2 Trace full-size flower and leaf patterns, *page 15*, onto paperbacked fusible webbing. Iron to reverse side of the coordinating fabrics, according to the manufacturer's directions. Cut out the fabric shapes. Using the placement diagram on *page 14* as a guide, fuse the flowers onto the tea cozy front according to the manufacturer's instructions. Machine-appliqué edges using matching threads.

3 Place the cozy front on top of a batting piece, and machine-quilt around the flowers and leaves. Use red embroidery floss to add French knots for detail. Sew on flower buttons where indicated. Cut out the quilted cozy front and plain back leaving a ½-inch seam allowance. Baste remaining batting piece to cozy back at edges. Trim batting around cozy shape.

4 Baste the red trim around the curved edge of the tea cozy front, aligning the straight edge of the trim with the marked edge of the tea cozy. Cut a 1½×1-inch piece of bias checked fabric for loop. Fold the piece lengthwise with right sides together. Stitch along the long edge using a ¼-inch seam allowance. Turn. Stitch the loop to the center of the cozy's top. Stitch the cozy front to the back with right sides facing. Clip seam. Turn.

5 Cut two lining pieces using the cozy pattern. Stitch rounded edge with right sides facing. Slip the lining fabric into cozy, matching side seams. Baste around bottom edge. Bind raw edges with a finished ¼-inch bias binding using checked fabric or purchased binding. To make binding, cut a strip of checked fabric on the bias approximately 1×26 inches. Fold in half lengthwise with wrong sides facing. With raw edges together, sew binding to bottom edge of cozy.

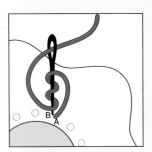

FRENCH KNOT DIAGRAM

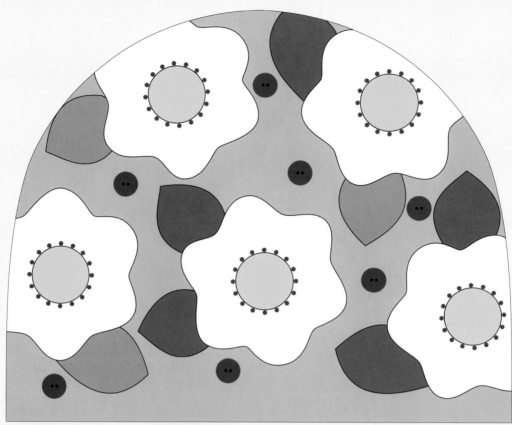

BLOOMING TEA COZY PLACEMENT DIAGRAM

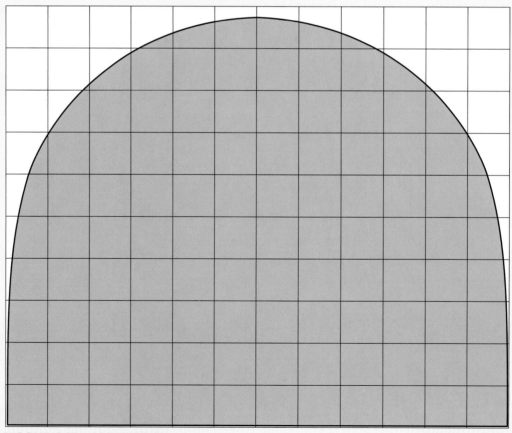

BLOOMING TEA COZY PATTERN

1 SQUARE = 1 INCH

14

BLOOMING TEA COZY FLOWER AND LEAF PATTERNS

sunshine bowl

Mary's favorite motifs turn an ordinary yellow mixing bowl into a striking work of art.

WHAT YOU'LL NEED
Yellow ceramic bowl
Tracing paper and pencil
Scissors
Glass paints in pink, red, green, black, and yellow
Fine- and medium-size round paintbrushes
Finepoint black paint marker
Black-and-white checked paper
Decoupage medium
Clear, waterproof varnish

HERE'S HOW

1 Purchase a yellow ceramic bowl that will tolerate the oven temperature of 325° if you choose to use bakeable glass paints. (You may use a glass paint that requires baking or one that does not. We suggest using the bowl for decoration only. If using the bowl for food, eliminate the painted design on the inside of the bowl.)

2 Trace the flower pattern, *right*, onto tracing paper. Cut out the pattern, and color the back of the tracing paper with a #2 pencil to transfer the design. Tape the pattern to the bowl, approximately ¼ inch from the rim. Draw over the design with a sharp pencil to transfer the pattern.

3 Paint the pink and red flowers and green leaves. Let them dry. Outline the painted design with a black paint marker. Let dry.

4 Cut a strip of black-and-white checked paper long enough to encircle the top of the bowl. Use the flower pattern to cut the ends where they will meet the painted design. Coat the back of the paper strip with decoupage medium, and apply to the rim of the bowl as shown, *right*. Let dry. Paint a coat of decoupage medium over the paper strip. Let dry. Wipe off excess from the bowl. Draw black lines at the top and bottom of the checked paper. Let dry.

5 Add black dots randomly around outside of bowl by dipping the handle tip of a paintbrush into paint and dotting the surface. Add small red flowers on the inside of the bowl. To do this, dip the eraser end of a pencil into red paint and dot the inside of the bowl. Let dry. Make small yellow dots in the center of each flower using the handle of a paintbrush.

6 Paint a coat of varnish over the decoupaged paper only. Let dry.

NOTE: *Do not immerse bowl in water. Wash and dry the inside of the bowl carefully; wipe the outside with a damp sponge when needed.*

PAINTED FLOWER
PATTERN

cherry-trimmed apron

Keep clean in the kitchen with this pretty apron which is as fresh as a summer breeze.

WHAT YOU'LL NEED

Apron pattern, such as McCall's #9334 view D; scissors
2 yards of 45-inch-wide, red-and-white plaid fabric
Matching threads
7 yards of red, extra-wide double-fold bias tape
8-inch or larger purchased doily
#5 red pearl cotton
4×12-inch piece of red cotton fabric
Tracing paper; pencil
Brown embroidery floss
4×4-inch pieces of two shades of green imitation suede fabric

HERE'S HOW

1 Cut and sew the apron according to the pattern. Trim edges using bias tape.

2 Cut the doily in half for pocket trims as shown in photograph, *opposite*. Turn the raw edge back and arrange a doily piece on each pocket; pin in place. Trim the edge of the doily on the pocket with blanket stitches using red pearl cotton. Blind-stitch the top of the doily to the top of the pocket.

3 Cut three 3-inch circles from red fabric. Make yo-yos by running a gathering stitch ¼-inch from the edge and pulling tight while tucking the raw edges under (*see page 37*). Trace the stem patterns and transfer to the apron front using a pencil. Stem-stitch the stems using three plies of brown embroidery floss.

4 Trace the full-size leaf patterns, *above*, onto tracing paper. Cut the leaf shapes from imitation suede. Machine-stitch the leaves to the apron using green thread through the leaf vein only. Hand-stitch the yo-yo cherries below the stems as shown *above*.

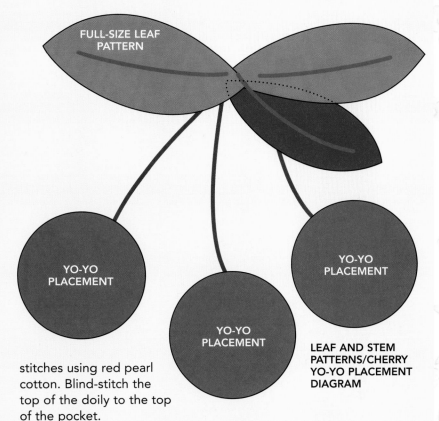

FULL-SIZE LEAF PATTERN

YO-YO PLACEMENT

YO-YO PLACEMENT

YO-YO PLACEMENT

LEAF AND STEM PATTERNS/CHERRY YO-YO PLACEMENT DIAGRAM

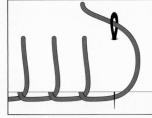

BLANKET STITCH

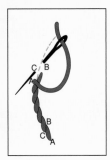

STEM STITCH

Serve sweet treats
from this celestial cake
stand trimmed with
dangling painted
cutouts and dainty
seed beads.

charmed goody plate

WHAT YOU'LL NEED

Tracing paper and pencil
10×10-inch piece of ¼-inch-thick
  wood; scroll saw
Fine sandpaper and tack cloth
Sanding sealer and paintbrush
Wood or glass candleholder or
  vase in desired shape for stem
All-purpose adhesive
Wood beads
Craft wire and wire clipper
Acrylic paints in medium and pale
  moss green, yellow, and red
Disposable foam or paper plate
Natural sponge
Purchased wood cutouts
  approximately 1 inch high:
  5 stars, 5 moons, and 5 hearts
Water-based, semi-gloss varnish
Ice pick
Fifteen 1-inch-long eye pins
Fifteen ½-inch-long eye pins
Needlenose pliers
Large black and white seed beads

HERE'S HOW

1 Enlarge and trace pattern, *below right*, onto tracing paper. Transfer the design to wood. Cut out and sand surfaces. Wipe with a tack cloth. Paint with a coat of sealer. Let dry.

2 Glue the candleholder or vase to the center of the wood plate top. Let dry.

3 Thread enough wood beads on craft wire to fit around base of stem. Secure the ends by twisting together. Clip off excess. Glue the circle of beads to the bottom of the stem. Let dry.

4 Paint the plate stand and beads using medium moss green. Let the paint dry. Use a small paintbrush to add pale moss green vertical and horizontal stripes to the stem center, if desired. Let dry.

5 Place a small amount of pale moss green paint on a disposable plate. Dampen the sponge with water. Dip sponge into paint and dab onto the surface of the plate stem where highlights are desired. Let dry.

6 Paint the moon and star shapes yellow. Paint the heart shapes red. Let dry.

7 Paint a coat of varnish on the plate stand and each wood shape. Let dry.

8 Use the ice pick to poke a hole in the center of each scallop edge. Poke a small hole in the top of each wood shape. If the shapes are too thin, eye pins can be glued to the backs.

9 Use pliers to bend each of the ½-inch-long eye pins to a 45-degree angle at the center. Open the loop on each eye pin.

10 Thread three alternating black and white seed beads on each 1-inch-long eye pin. Glue the end in the top hole or on the top back of each wood shape. Let dry. Connect a ½-inch-long eye pin to each 1-inch-long pin. Close loop. Glue the ends of the ½-inch pins in the side holes of the plate top. Let dry.

Note: Place a clear glass plate or doily lined with waxed paper on top of the stand before using.

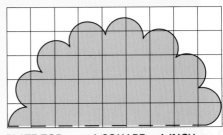

PLATE TOP
PATTERN   1 SQUARE = 1 INCH

stirring spoons

Embellish mismatched flea market silverware by creating fresh-looking clay flowers to adorn the handles.

WHAT YOU'LL NEED

Spoons or other desired silverware

Bakeable clay, such as Sculpey, in yellow, red, blue, purple, and green

Small sharp knife

Glass baking dish

Toothpick

Strong adhesive, such as E6000

HERE'S HOW

1 Wash the silverware. Let it dry.

2 To make the yellow flower, roll a piece of clay into a ball about the size of a small grape. Flatten it gently with your finger. Make a smaller red ball for the center. Gently flatten it onto the center of the yellow ball. Make the red flower the same way as the yellow flower, but use a smaller pea-size ball of clay and a very small yellow center.

3 To make the blue flower, roll five small balls about ³⁄₁₆ inch in diameter. Arrange into a circle. Press down in the center to adhere them together. Arrange five smaller yellow balls in the center, and press down. Gently press a tiny red ball in the center.

4 To make the purple flower, roll a piece of clay into a ball about the size of a medium grape. Flatten it gently. Use a knife to press six lines into the top, as shown, to make separate petals.

5 To shape a leaf, form a small oval and flatten. Gently press a crease down the middle of leaf with the edge of a knife. Press leaf shapes onto flowers where desired.

6 Place the clay pieces in a glass baking dish. Bake in oven according to the product instructions. Let cool.

7 Use a toothpick to apply adhesive to the back of each flower. Press onto silverware handle ends. Let dry.

Note: Do not soak, scrub, or put clay-embellished silverware in dishwasher.

nighty-night

When the stars and the moon shine brilliantly in the dark sky, we turn to our private havens and say nighty-night to the world. This chapter offers comforting quilts and pillows along with adorable accents to make every bedroom in the house a lovingly furnished retreat.

This pair of pretty quilted pillows will add color and charm to make your house home sweet home.

WHAT YOU'LL NEED

For the patchwork pillow

Tracing paper and pencil; scissors

½ yard of 45-inch-wide yellow stripe fabric for border and backing

¼ yard each of red, yellow plaid, and blue checked fabric

⅛ yard each of black, white, and yellow plaid fabric

2 yards of narrow black sew-in piping

Matching quilting threads

17×17-inch piece of fleece

16×16-inch pillow form

For the flower appliqué pillow

Tracing paper and pencil; scissors

½ yard of 45-inch-wide blue print for background and back

¼ yard of yellow print for petals

¼ yard of yellow stripe for border

⅛ yard of green print for leaves

⅛ yard of red print for triangles

6×6-inch piece of contrasting red print for center circle

3×12-inch piece of contrasting yellow plaid for corners

Paperbacked fusible webbing

Matching threads

#3 pearl cotton in green, gold, and yellow for French knots

2 yards of narrow black sew-in piping

17×17-inch piece of fleece

16×16-inch pillow form

HERE'S HOW

For the patchwork pillow

1 Trace and cut out the full-size patterns, *page 28*. Cut the following, which include a ¼-inch seam allowance:

  8 black squares, each 1½×1½ inches

  8 white squares, each 1½×1½ inches

  4 blue checked squares, each 4½×4½ inches

  4 yellow print triangles

  4 red triangles

  4 yellow stripe borders, each 2½×12½ inches

  4 contrasting plaid corners, each 2½×2½ inches

  16½×16½-inch backing fabric

2 Piece and stitch patchwork according to placement diagram on *page 28*. Press. Line patchwork with fleece. Machine-quilt ¼ inch from seams with matching thread. Stitch piping around outside edge. Stitch front to back, right sides together, leaving an opening for turning. Trim corners and turn. Insert pillow form. Stitch opening closed.

For the flower appliqué pillow

1 Trace and cut out the full-size patterns, *page 29*. Cut the following, which include a ¼-inch seam allowance:

  1 blue background, 12½×12½ inches

  4 red triangles

  8 large yellow petals

  8 small yellow petals

  6 green leaves

  4 yellow stripe borders, each 2½×12½ inches

  4 contrasting yellow plaid corners, each 2½×2½ inches

  16½×16½-inch backing fabric

continued on page 28

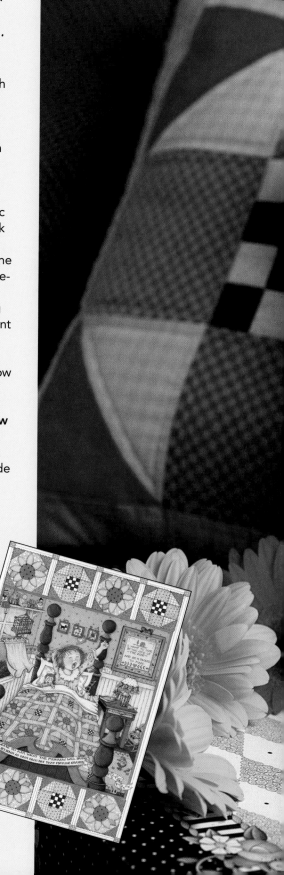

TRIANGLE PATTERN

1½-INCH SQUARE PATTERN

PATCHWORK PILLOW PATTERNS

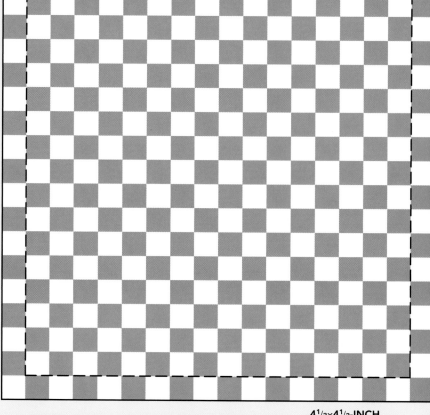

4½×4½-INCH SQUARE PATTERN

country quilted pillows — *continued*

2 Stitch the red corners to the blue background. Cut off points of blue fabric. Stitch four pairs each of large and small petals along the curved edges, leaving the straight edge open. Clip the seam and turn. Press. Repeat with leaves.

3 Arrange and pin large petals vertically and horizontally. Add small petals and leaves.

4 Trace the circle pattern onto webbing. Fuse to wrong side of red fabric. Cut out and fuse in the center of petals. Machine-satin-stitch around the edge using matching thread.

5 Attach edges of leaves and petals to blue background with pearl cotton using French knots.

6 Complete piecing of pillow top the same as the patchwork pillow. Line the top with fleece and machine-quilt around the petals and leaves. Finish in the same manner as the patchwork pillow.

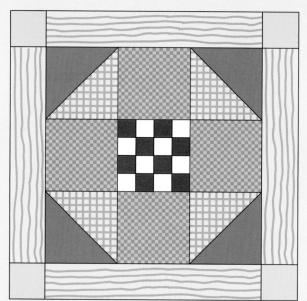

PATCHWORK PILLOW PLACEMENT DIAGRAM

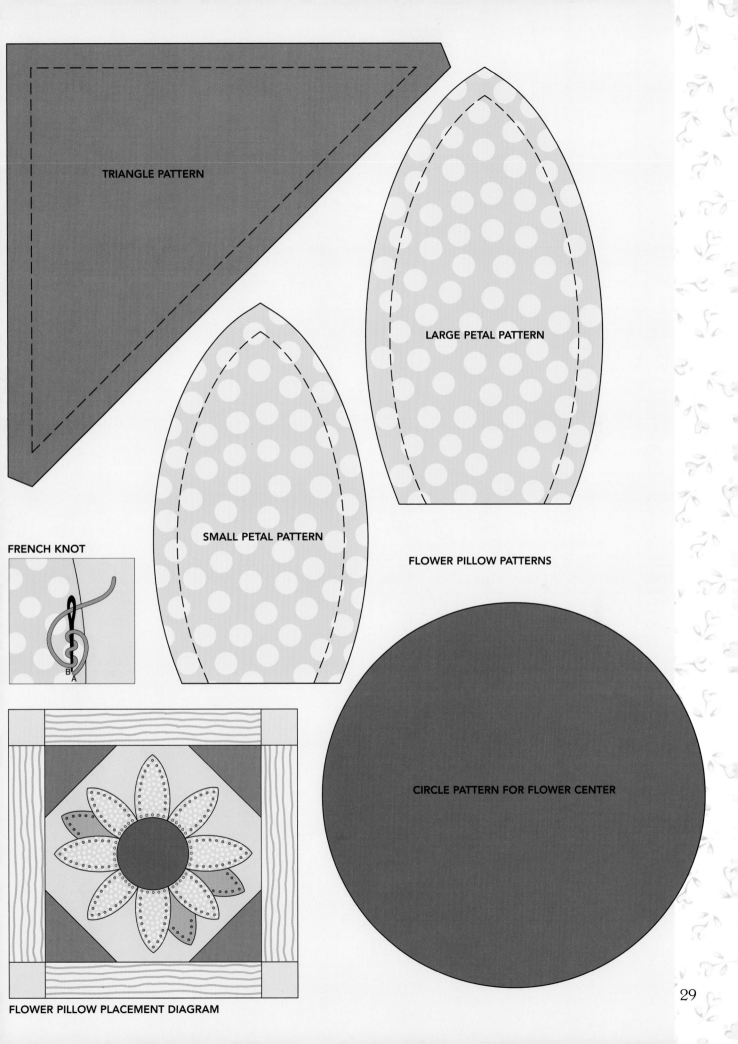

TRIANGLE PATTERN

LARGE PETAL PATTERN

SMALL PETAL PATTERN

FLOWER PILLOW PATTERNS

FRENCH KNOT

B A

CIRCLE PATTERN FOR FLOWER CENTER

FLOWER PILLOW PLACEMENT DIAGRAM

fun framed trio

Bordered in bright red frames, these clay creations display a host of textures enhanced with brilliant paints. Turn the page to learn how to make this clever trio.

fun framed trio — *continued*

WHAT YOU'LL NEED
Three 5×5-inch frames
Cardboard
Scissors
Tracing paper
Pencil
White bakeable clay, such
   as Sculpey
Small sharp knife
Glass baking dish
Paintbrush
Thick white crafts glue
Acrylic gel medium; toothpick
Acrylic paints in black, white,
   sky blue, green, yellow, brown,
   and red; black leather cording
Gloss varnish

HERE'S HOW

1 Cut a 5×5-inch piece of cardboard for each picture base. Set aside.

2 Trace the patterns, *right* and *opposite*, onto tracing paper. Use the patterns as guides by shaping the clay on top of the pattern.

3 *To make the dog,* work in sections. Roll an oblong piece and place over the areas on the drawing. Fill in body area, head, and tail. Smooth all pieces together to form a uniform piece.

3 Create hair texture using a small sharp knife.

4 *To make the sunflower,* begin each petal with a small ball. Flatten the ball, pinch the end to a point, and make a crease down the center using a knife. Make several petals and arrange as shown on the pattern. Roll a golf-ball size piece of clay and flatten it for the center. Make indentations with the handle of a paintbrush.

5 *To make the cherries,* roll a ball of dough the size of a small walnut, and flatten it slightly. Press the pointed end of a pencil into cherries where stems will attach. Shape an oblong or oval

shape for the leaves. Pinch the ends and flatten. Make a center vein crease using a knife pressed flat against the clay.

6 Remove pattern from clay shapes. Bake clay on a glass baking dish according to product instructions. Let cool.

7 To create the textured backgrounds, paint the cardboard squares with a medium flat paintbrush and acrylic gel medium. Apply it heavily in deeply textured areas such as the grass on the dog picture.

DOG PATTERN

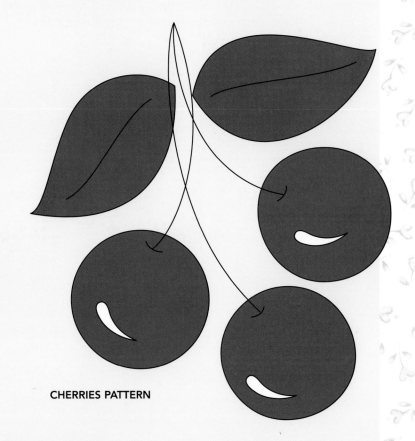

CHERRIES PATTERN

8 Make the grass using a toothpick to draw lines. Position clay dog in grass, and let dry until firm. Other pieces may be glued onto gel-prepared boards.

9 Paint each piece, using the patterns as guides. Let dry. Use black leather cord for the cherry stems. Cut to desired length and glue in place. Coat each piece generously with glossy varnish. Let dry.

10 If desired, paint the frames red, and let dry. Add a coat of varnish. Let dry. Insert the pictures into the frames.

SUNFLOWER PATTERN

Yo-yo flowers and ribbon accents make this a stunning quilt a girl will cherish forever.

34

cuddle-up quilt

WHAT YOU'LL NEED

Tracing paper; pencil; scissors

1½ yards of 45-inch-wide peach print for ribbon diamonds

1½ yards of 45-inch-wide peach gingham for diamonds and triangles

1¾ yards of 45-inch-wide green print for sashing

4 yards of 45-inch-wide yellow print for border, back, and binding

½ yard of 45-inch-wide green stripe print for pieced border

½ yard of 45-inch-wide pink checked print for pieced border

1 yard of gold print for attached diamonds

½ yard of rose print for yo-yo flowers

40 yards of ⅛-inch-wide strawberry satin ribbon for diamond accents

35 yards of ¼-inch-wide gold grosgrain ribbon for diamond borders

4 yards of 1-inch-wide green grosgrain ribbon for border

¼ yard of 72-inch-wide green felt for leaves

22 yellow ¾-inch-diameter shank buttons

Batting; thread

HERE'S HOW

1 Enlarge and trace the quilt patterns on *page 37*, to cut the following which include a ¼-inch seam allowance:

  15 peach print diamonds from pattern piece A

  8 peach gingham diamonds from pattern piece A

  8 peach gingham triangles from pattern piece B

  4 peach gingham triangles from pattern piece C

  2 peach gingham triangles from pattern piece D and 2 from pattern piece

D, reversed (Dr on diagram)

Cut green print sashing fabric lengthwise as necessary into 2-inch-wide strips

44 gold print appliqué diamonds from pattern piece E

22 rose print 5-inch-diameter circles for yo-yo flowers

22 green felt leaves from pattern piece F

Cut yellow print border 6½×60½ inches

60 green stripe print squares, each 2½×2½ inches

60 pink checked print squares, each 2½×2½ inches

2 Topstitch the strawberry satin ribbon onto the peach print diamonds 1½ inches apart according to the diagram, *page 37*.

3 Set quilt pieces together in checkerboard fashion in diagonal rows, stitching a green print sashing strip between the diamonds. After stitching each sashing strip, trim into diamond shape at points. Stitch opposite diagonal rows together with a long continuous green sashing strip.

4 Topstitch gold grosgrain ribbon along green sashing strips in a diagonal grid pattern.

5 Stitch yellow border at the top and bottom edges of the quilt. Set pieced border together in checkerboard fashion for two rows with the green stripe print and pink checked print fabric. Stitch to yellow border. Stitch green ribbon onto yellow border along seam line of pieced diamonds.

6 Piece backing fabric. Layer backing fabric batting and quilt top. Baste together. Quilt as desired.

continued on page 36

cuddle-up quilt — *continued*

7 Bind edge with ⅜-inch-wide finished double-fold binding. Stitch gold print appliqué diamonds together in pairs, right sides facing, with a ¼-inch seam. Trim corners. Make a small slit in one side of diamond pair. Turn diamond to right side through slit. Press.

8 Make 22 yo-yos from rose print circles by gathering outside edge and pulling thread tight as shown, *opposite*. Layer yo-yo and leaves at center of each gold print diamond. Sew button through all layers to secure. Machine-tack or hand-tack flower diamonds to quilt.

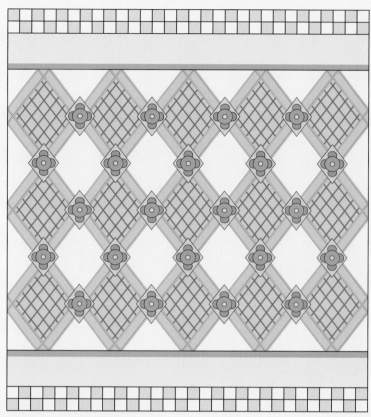

QUILT PLACEMENT DIAGRAM

QUILT DETAILS

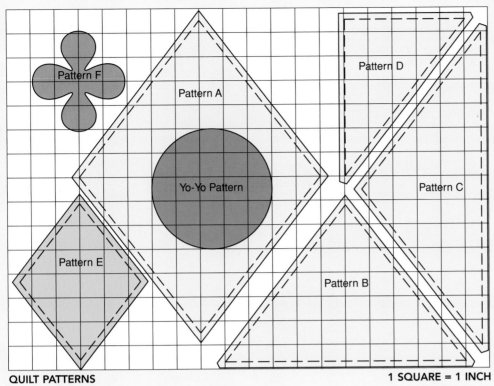

QUILT PATTERNS

Pattern F

Pattern D

Pattern A

Pattern C

Yo-Yo Pattern

Pattern E

Pattern B

1 SQUARE = 1 INCH

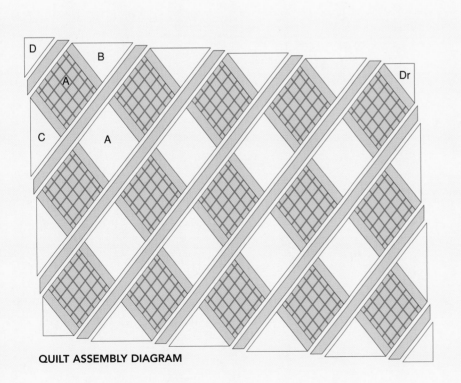

D

B

A

Dr

C

A

QUILT ASSEMBLY DIAGRAM

YO-YO DIAGRAMS

free-flying mobile

A sweet addition to any bedroom, this clever mobile whirls and twirls with each gentle breeze.

WHAT YOU'LL NEED

Tracing paper; pencil
Scissors
Papier-mâché egg
Air-dry clay, such as Crayola Model Magic; rolling pin
Toothpicks
Push pin
Medium flat and fine paintbrushes
Acrylic paints in orange, light blue, yellow, medium blue, red, green, white, pink, and black
24-inch piece of beading string
Black seed beads
Clear gloss varnish

HERE'S HOW

1 Trace the full-size patterns, *pages 40–41*, onto tracing paper and cut out.

2 *To make the bird and heart,* flatten a tangerine-size piece of clay with a rolling pin to about ¼-inch thick. Lay the patterns for the bird wings and tail and for the heart onto the clay. Trace around the patterns with a pencil.

Cut out the pieces with scissors. Use a toothpick to pierce a hole through the center of the heart for stringing. Insert toothpicks into the wings, tail, and head so they can be inserted into egg body when dry. Shape a large marble-size ball for the bird's head and a cone shape for the beak. Let the clay pieces dry.

With a pushpin, pierce holes into sides of the egg and at each end for attaching wings, tail, and head. Also pierce holes through the center of the egg for stringing.

Assemble the bird, gluing clay pieces in place. Let the glue dry. Paint the bird's belly orange and the rest of the body light blue. Paint the beak yellow. Paint the heart red. Let dry. To make medium blue dots on the bird and white dots on the heart, dip the handle tip of a small paintbrush in paint and dot onto surface. Let dry.

3 *To make a bee,* roll out various sized balls as shown on *page 40* and flatten. Gently press wings, body, and head together. Let dry. Paint wings white and body and head yellow. Let dry. Paint small pink spots on white wings and three black stripes on the body. Let dry.

4 *To make a flower,* flatten a golf-ball-size piece of clay as shown on *page 41*. Make smaller balls for the center and leaves and flatten. Gently press pieces together and let dry. Paint the flower red, the center yellow, and the leaves green. Let dry.

5 Spray all clay shapes with clear gloss varnish. Let dry.

6 Insert the beading thread through the needle. Thread and knot one bead on the end. Insert thread through the bottom of the heart upward. String about an inch of black beads. Thread the bee, more beads, the bird, more beads, the flower, and more beads. Finish the end by making a loop of strung beads and tying string in a knot to secure the loop.

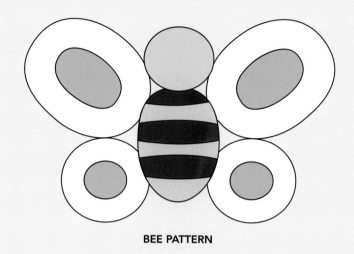

BEE PATTERN

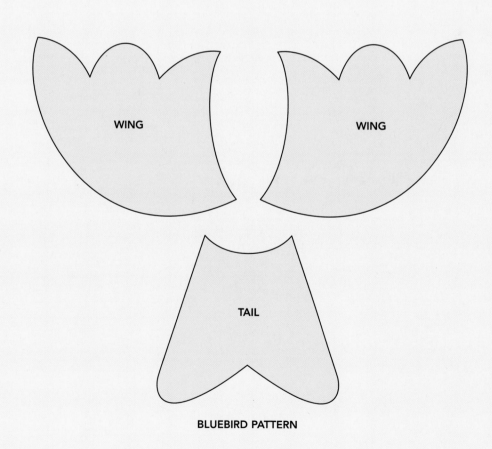

WING

WING

TAIL

BLUEBIRD PATTERN

FLOWER PATTERN

HEART PATTERN

cheerful pillow sham

WHAT YOU'LL NEED

Scissors

½ yard of black-and-white checked fabric for background

¼ yard of white fabric for border

1 yard of black fabric for border and backing

Paperbacked fusible webbing

⅛ yard each of rose fabric for corner flowers, blue fabric for center flowers, and green fabric for leaves

2×10-inch piece of contrasting rose fabric for flower centers

Embroidery floss in black, green, and blue

Rose and green threads for machine appliqué

2 yards of ⅜-inch-wide rose grosgrain ribbon

24×20-inch piece of fleece

Six ⅞-inch-diameter yellow sew-through buttons

#3 rose pearl cotton

3 yards of narrow black sew-in piping

HERE'S HOW

1 Cut the following (each piece includes a ¼-inch seam allowance):

14½×18½-inch black-and-white checked fabric for background

114 white squares, each 1½×1½ inches

114 black squares, each 1½×1½ inches

2 black pieces of fabric, each 18¼×20½ for back

2 Mark a 14×18-inch rectangle in the center of the black-and-white checked background fabric. Trace the flowers and leaves patterns, *page 44*, onto paperbacked fusible webbing. Fuse to fabrics according to the manufacturer's instructions. Cut out and fuse to the background fabric according to the pattern.

3 Work two-ply blanket stitches around the flowers and leaves as shown on *page 44*. Machine-satin-stitch leaf veins and rose flower centers with matching threads.

4 Piece black and white squares in checkerboard fashion in three rows for border. Baste border over appliqué. Top-stitch rose ribbon over raw edges, and miter at corners.

5 Line top with fleece. Machine-quilt around flowers and leaves. Sew buttons on blue flowers, and add French knots to rose flowers. Stitch piping around outside edge of pillow. Press and stitch a double 1-inch hem along one short side of the two sham back pieces. Overlap hemmed edges to match same size as front. Stitch front to back, right sides facing. Trim corners. Turn to right side. Insert pillow.

THERE'S ABSOLUTELY NO REASON TO BE RUSHED ALONG WITH THE RUSH. —ROBERT FROST

The intricate details of this beautiful
machine-quilted sham make it an heirloom-to-be.
The patterns are on page 44.

43

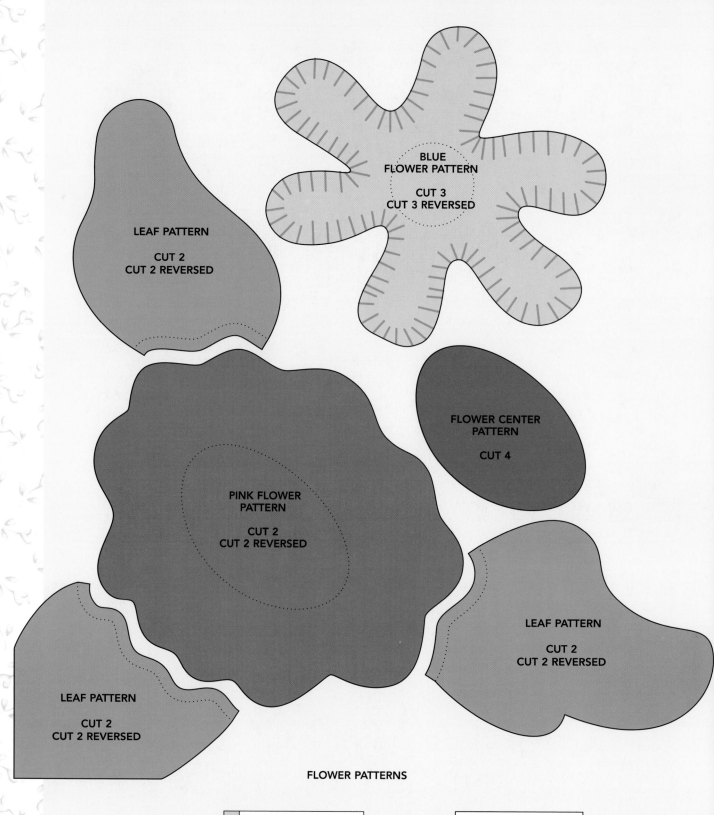

BLUE
FLOWER PATTERN

CUT 3
CUT 3 REVERSED

LEAF PATTERN

CUT 2
CUT 2 REVERSED

FLOWER CENTER
PATTERN

CUT 4

PINK FLOWER
PATTERN

CUT 2
CUT 2 REVERSED

LEAF PATTERN

CUT 2
CUT 2 REVERSED

LEAF PATTERN

CUT 2
CUT 2 REVERSED

FLOWER PATTERNS

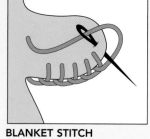

BLANKET STITCH

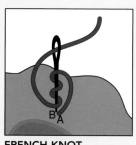

FRENCH KNOT

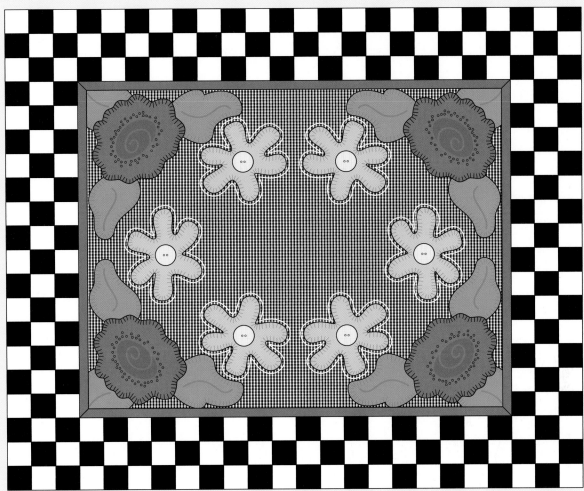

PILLOW SHAM PLACEMENT DIAGRAM

PILLOW SHAM DETAIL

adorable dresser scarf

This scarf can easily be adapted to any size by altering the length of the center stripes to add a soft touch to any nightstand or dresser.

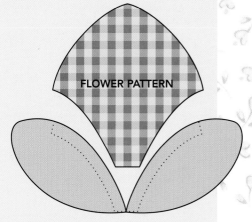

FLOWER PATTERN

WHAT YOU'LL NEED
1 yard of rose print fabric for border and backing
¼ yard of pink checked fabric for piecing strips
¾ yard green fabric for piecing strips, binding, and leaves
⅛ yard rose gingham for flowers
3½ yards medium pink rickrack
Matching threads
17×30-inch piece of fleece
Paperbacked fusible webbing

HERE'S HOW
1 Cut the following (each piece includes a ¼-inch seam allowance):
4 green strips, each 2×17 inches
3 pink check strips, each 3½×17 inches
2 green border pieces, each 2×15½ inches
2 rose print border pieces, each 5×15½ inches with scallops as shown on pattern, *below right*
2 Piece the center of the scarf as shown on the placement diagram, *right*. Stitch rickrack on

pink. Add a green border at each end. Add rose print border pieces. Using pattern for scalloped border, trim rose print border fabric to match.
3 Trace 10 flower shapes onto paperbacked fusible webbing. Fuse to the rose gingham according to the manufacturer's instructions. Repeat with 20 green leaves. Cut out and fuse to the border. Line top with fleece.
4 Cut backing fabric same as front. Stitch along sides, right

sides together. Turn to the right side. Machine-quilt seam lines. Satin-stitch flowers and leaves in matching threads.
5 Bind scallops with green ½-inch finished bias binding.

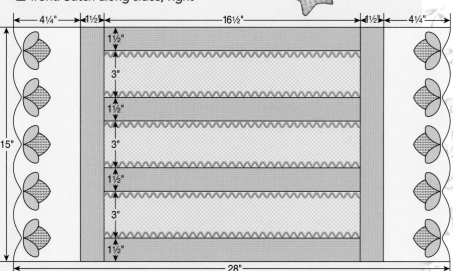

DRESSER SCARF PLACEMENT DIAGRAM

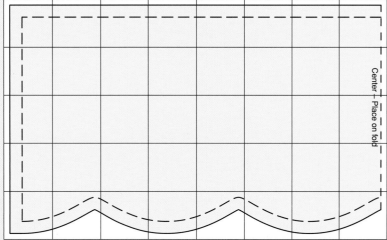

SCALLOPED BORDER PATTERN   **1 SQUARE = 1 INCH**

Center — Place on fold

sweet little rooms

I t's the unexpected accents that turn the small spaces in your home into sweet little rooms. Whether you enjoy quilting, painting, or hand embroidery, you're sure to find a project you love in this chapter— one that will display your personality and creativity in your favorite corner of the house.

felt penny pillow

Like a vintage penny rug, a rainbow of felt circles dances on this pillow's midnight black background.

WHAT YOU'LL NEED
Tracing paper; pencil
18×18-inch piece of black felt for background
9×12-inch piece of felt in each of the following colors: pink, orange, red, burgundy, aqua, turquoise, purple, gold, yellow, and yellow gold
Two 9×12-inch pieces of olive green felt for leaves
Matching embroidery floss
Poly-fil
2 yards of gold sew-in piping cord
18×18-inch piece of calico for back
18×18-inch piece of interfacing
#5 red pearl cotton
15×15-inch pillow form

HERE'S HOW
1 Measure and mark a 15×15-inch square in the center of the black square of felt.

2 Trace full-size patterns, *page 53*, onto tracing paper and cut out. Use pattern to cut various sizes of circles from felt colors as desired. Cut 20 green felt leaves.

3 Using the placement diagram, *page 52*, as a guide, pin several large circles to the black background. Blanket-stitch around each circle with three plies of matching floss (see diagram on *page 53*). Tuck leaves under circles before completing stitches. Overlap circles and leaves as necessary to make design fit. Trim short side of leaf as necessary to make various sizes.

4 Layer a contrasting small or medium circle onto the large circles, and blanket stitch around the edges. Before completing blanket stitches around the top circles, stuff with a pinch of poly-fil. Fill in open spaces with medium and small circles.

5 Trim the pillow to ½ inch past the 15×15-inch mark. Stitch piping on marked edge. Interface calico for back, and cut to same size as front.

6 Stitch pillow front to back, right sides facing. Leave an opening for turning. Turn to right side. Insert pillow form. Stitch opening closed. To add cording, whipstitch (see diagram on *page 53*) every ¼ inch to edges using two plies of red pearl cotton.

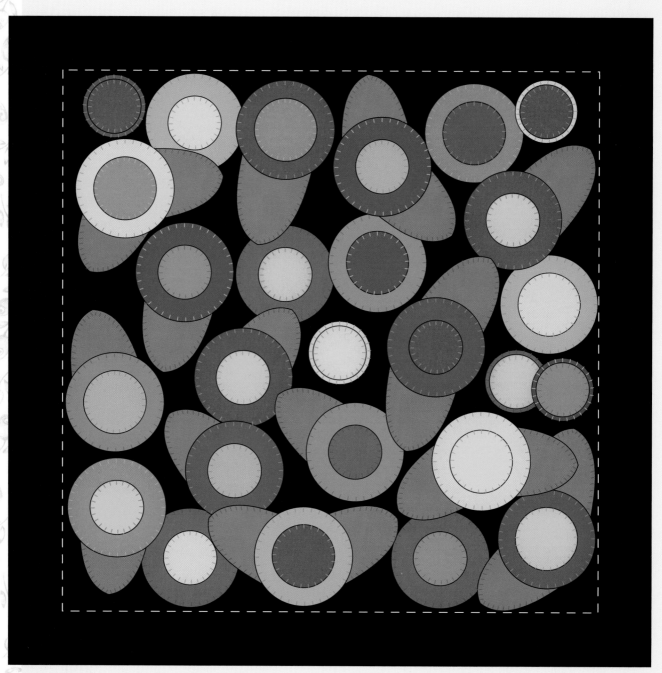

FELT PENNIES PILLOW PLACEMENT DIAGRAM

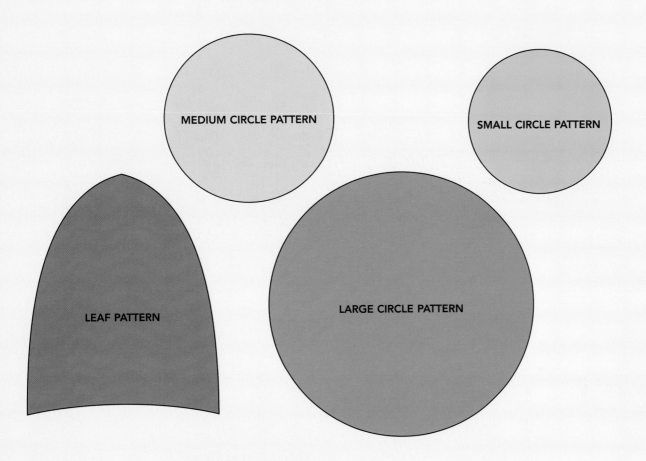

MEDIUM CIRCLE PATTERN

SMALL CIRCLE PATTERN

LEAF PATTERN

LARGE CIRCLE PATTERN

FELT PENNIES PILLOW PATTERNS

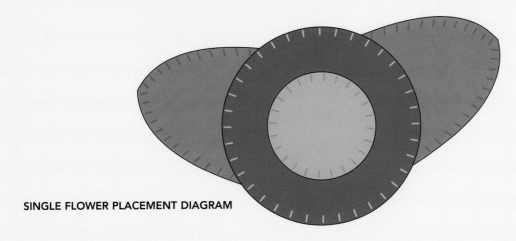

SINGLE FLOWER PLACEMENT DIAGRAM

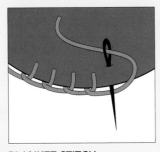

BLANKET STITCH

WHIP STITCH

forever flowers

Sprouting cheerfully from a polka-dot painted vase, these felt flowers bloom all year long.

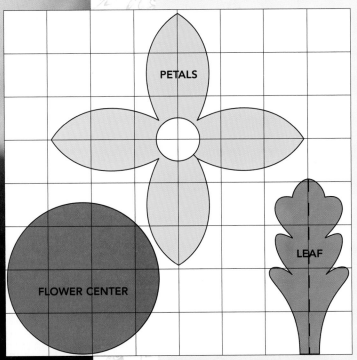

WHAT YOU'LL NEED
Tracing paper; pencil; scissors
¼ yard of yellow-green and
  yellow felt for petals
One 8×11-inch piece of red
  felt for flower centers
One 5×9-inch piece of
  green felt for leaves
Green floral tape
Poly-fil; thread; awl
6 medium-weight cotton-
  wrapped stem wires, each
  18 inches long
Six ¾-inch yellow shank buttons
Six 1-inch sew-through buttons
Needlenose pliers; yellow vase
Orange-red acrylic paint
Pencil with round eraser

HERE'S HOW

1 Enlarge and trace patterns, *below,* and cut out. Cut petals from yellow and yellow-green felt. Cut a red circle for each flower center. Cut leaves from green felt.

2 Cut center circle from a group of petals. Make a cut through one petal section. Repeat with a second group of petals, removing one petal. Gather the seven petals and connect into a continuous circle. Secure with thread.

3 Gather the outside edge of each red circle to make a yo-yo as shown on *page 37.* Stuff with poly-fil. Make a 4-inch hook on one end of the stem wire using pliers. With an awl, poke a hole in center of yo-yo. Thread yellow button onto wire hook. Slip long and short ends of the wire through the hole in the yo-yo, adding gathered petals. Slip button through long and short ends of wire, and twist to secure.

4 Press leaves in half lengthwise. Cut 3½-inch pieces of wire. Place wire in center of each leaf and wrap with floral tape. Wrap stem with tape, adding leaf section.

5 For vase, dip the eraser end of a pencil into paint and dot onto the surface. Let the paint dry.

PETALS

LEAF

FLOWER CENTER

FLOWER AND LEAF PATTERNS
1 SQUARE = 1 INCH

polka-dot tick-tock

WHAT YOU'LL NEED
Mantle clock
Masking tape, optional
Sandpaper and tack cloth
White spray primer
Acrylic paints in sky blue, red,
 white, black, yellow, orange,
 and green
Paintbrushes; tracing paper
Pencil with round eraser
Acrylic semigloss sealer

HERE'S HOW

1 Remove the clock face or cover it with masking tape. Lightly sand the clock, and wipe the dust away with a tack cloth. Spray on a light coat of primer. Let it dry. Apply a second coat if necessary. Let it dry.

2 If the clock has a base like this one, paint the sides of the base white. Let the paint dry. Paint the top of the base red. Let dry. Measure and mark off sides to paint a checkerboard design. Paint every other square black as shown, alternating on two or more rows. Let the paint dry.

3 Paint the remaining sections of the clock sky blue. Let the paint dry.

4 Trace the large flower pattern, *right,* onto tracing paper. Color the back side of the tracing paper with pencil.

5 Transfer the design to each side of the clock face, reversing the pattern for the left side.

6 Paint the flower sections red. Let the paint dry.

7 To make red dots around clock face, dip the eraser of a pencil into paint and dot onto surface. Paint the stems and leaves green. Let dry. Add tiny white dots between each

larger red dot by dipping the handle tip of a paintbrush into paint and dotting onto the surface. Add vertical rows of tiny dots to both sides of clock face.

8 Add flowers to the clock top using a pencil eraser dipped in paint. Use yellow, red, and orange for the flowers. Make yellow and red centers using the handle end of a paintbrush. Use a small round paintbrush to make green oval leaves.

9 Add tiny white and green dots between flowers as desired. Let the paint dry.

10 Apply a coat of sealer to the painted areas. Let dry. Remove masking tape, or replace the clock face.

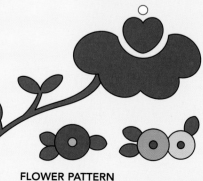

FLOWER PATTERN

*Checking the time
will be a pleasure with
this hand-painted
beauty by your bedside.* 57

lined-up bookends

WHAT YOU'LL NEED

8 thick hardcover books in
  uniform size and shape
White spray primer
Medium flat and fine liner
  paintbrushes
Acrylic paints in yellow, orange,
  ochre, pale yellow, lime
  green, dark green, white, soft
  green, red, bright yellow, baby
  blue, bright blue, black, pink,
  and purple; tracing paper; pencil
Clear gloss varnish

HERE'S HOW

1 Plan the design for each
  book before beginning to
paint. Refer to the patterns,
pages 60–61, for ideas. In a
well-ventilated work area, spray
primer on the front, back, and
binding of each book. Let dry.

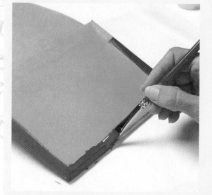

2 Paint the solid background
  colors first. Open the book

and paint around the inside
edges neatly so it looks
completely painted when the
book is closed. Let dry. If there
are embossed designs on the
spines of the books, use them
as guides to create blocks of
color. Paint the blocks of color
as desired, painting over the
background color. Let dry.

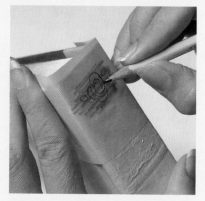

3 To paint the large flowers or
  heart designs, trace the
desired patterns, *pages 60–61*,
onto tracing paper. Color the

continued on page 60

Castaway books are given a fresh new look by painting the spines with tiny motifs. Group them together, stacked or side-by-side, to make one-of-a-kind bookends.

59

lined-up bookends — *continued*

back of tracing paper with a soft or #2 pencil. Tape the pattern in position and draw around outline with a sharp pencil to transfer the pattern onto the book.

4 Paint the details inside the color blocks. For outlined blocks, use a fine liner paintbrush. Paint stripes where desired.

5 To make checks, use a fine liner brush or a very small flat paintbrush.

6 To make dots, dip the handle tip of paintbrush into paint and dot onto surface. You can use a pencil eraser to make flowers by dipping into paint and dotting onto surface.

7 When finished painting, apply two coats of clear gloss varnish, allowing to dry between coats.

GARDEN BOUQUET BOOKEND

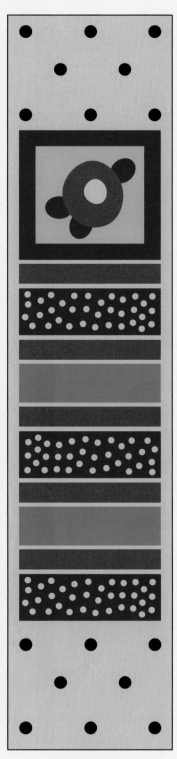

SINGLE BLOOM BOOKEND

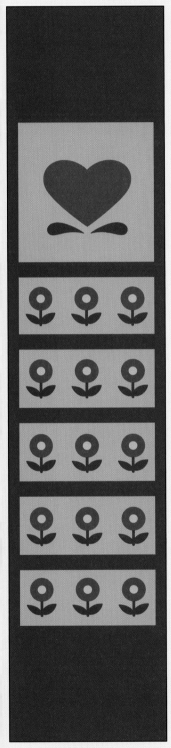

**FLOWERS-IN-A-ROW
BOOKEND**

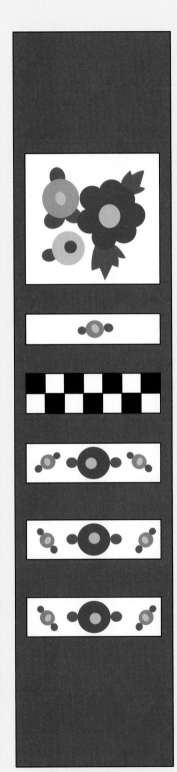

**BRILLIANT BLOOMS
BOOKEND**

**FLOWERS 'N' VINES
BOOKEND**

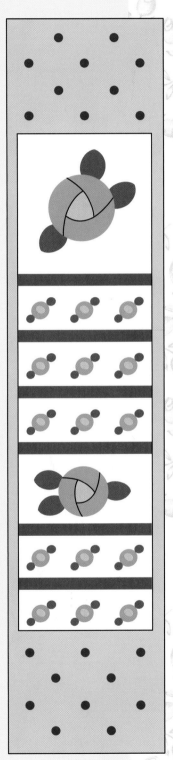

**PINK BLOSSOM
BOOKEND**

ring-of-tulips pillow

A layer of sheer organdy rests atop the pastel tulip design to add a softness to this shadow-quilted pillow.

WHAT YOU'LL NEED
Tracing paper and pencil
Scissors
Paperbacked fusible webbing
⅛ yard of bright pink fabric for
  flowers
⅛ yard of green fabric for
  leaves
18×18-inch piece of fleece
18×18-inch piece of gold print
  for background
Matching threads
18×18-inch piece of sheer white
  organdy fabric
1¼ yards of blue-and-white
  checked fabric for back
  and ruffle
2½-inch-diameter button form
2 yards of narrow piping cord
14-inch round pillow form

HERE'S HOW

1 Trace the full-size patterns, *page 65,* onto tracing paper and cut out. Trace six flowers and six leaves onto paperbacked fusible webbing. Fuse to the corresponding fabrics following the manufacturer's instructions. Cut out. Cut a 15-inch circle from gold print fabric. Fuse the shapes to the circle as shown on placement diagram, *page 64.*

2 Line pillow top with fleece. Place organdy over pillow top, and baste together around edge. Machine-quilt through all layers at outer edge of flowers and leaves. Machine-quilt stems, separating from leaves as shown.

3 Cut back same size as front from blue-and-white checked fabric. Cut ruffle on bias 4½ inches wide by twice the circumference of the pillow, piecing as necessary.

4 Cut a 1-inch-wide bias strip and cover piping. Stitch piping around top circle. Trim circle, leaving ½-inch seam allowance. Press ruffle in half lengthwise, wrong sides facing. Stitch gathering thread to raw edges. Gather and stitch ruffle to piping. Stitch front to back leaving an opening for turning. Trim seam allowance. Clip seam. Turn to right side.

5 Insert pillow form. Stitch opening closed. Cover button and stitch to center of pillow.

RING-OF-TULIPS PILLOW PLACEMENT DIAGRAM

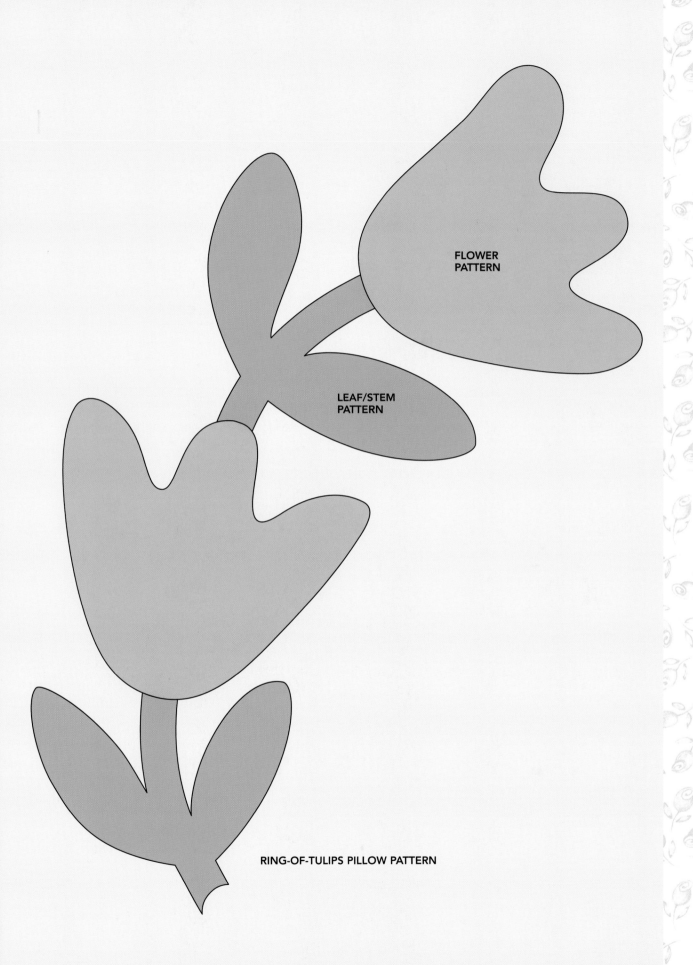

FLOWER
PATTERN

LEAF/STEM
PATTERN

RING-OF-TULIPS PILLOW PATTERN

pretty patchwork bag

This handy drawstring bag has a surprise inside—a flower bottom stitched with pockets to hold a comb, jewelry, cotton swabs, and more.

WHAT YOU'LL NEED
Tracing paper
Pencil
Scissors
26×26-inch piece of white fabric
Fabric scraps for patchwork
Matching rayon threads
2 yards of narrow white piping
  cord
24×24-inch piece of gold print
  for lining
⅛ yard of bright pink calico
2 yards of blue cord; button

HERE'S HOW

1 Center and trace a 24-inch circle onto the white fabric for base. Using the diagram on *page 69* for ideas, make a crazy patchwork piece from fabric scraps, allowing enough fabric to cover the circle.

2 When base fabric is completely patched, machine-baste on the traced line. Cut out just beyond stitching. With two rayon threads in top of machine, or by hand, embroider with a decorative stitch around the patches as desired.

3 Stitch piping ½ inch in from the outside edge.

4 Cut lining fabric same size as patchwork. Trace full-size flower pattern, *page 69*. Cut two flowers. Cut a 5-inch circle from desired fabric for yo-yo. Fold patchwork circle in half and mark two ¾-inch button holes on fold, each 1¾ inch from the raw edge.

5 Stitch patchwork to lining, right sides facing. Leave an opening for turning. Clip seam as necessary. Turn to right side. Stitch opening closed. Machine-topstitch a circle 1¾ inches from outer edge. Machine-topstitch another circle ¾ inch from first circle to create a casing for cord.

6 Stitch flower pieces together, right sides facing. Clip seam. Make a small slit at the center of one piece. Turn and press. Machine-embroider or hand-sew a decorative stitch around the outside edge. Center the flower onto the lining. Machine-topstitch flower on lines from pattern to create pockets.

continued on page 68

pretty patchwork bag — *continued*

7 Make a yo-yo from the small circle by running a gathering stitch around the outside edge and pulling thread tight. Hand-stitch to center of flower. Sew a button to the center of the yo-yo. Cut cord into two 1-yard lengths. Thread cords through buttonholes, each from a different side. Knot ends of cord. Glue to secure.

BAG INSIDE DETAIL

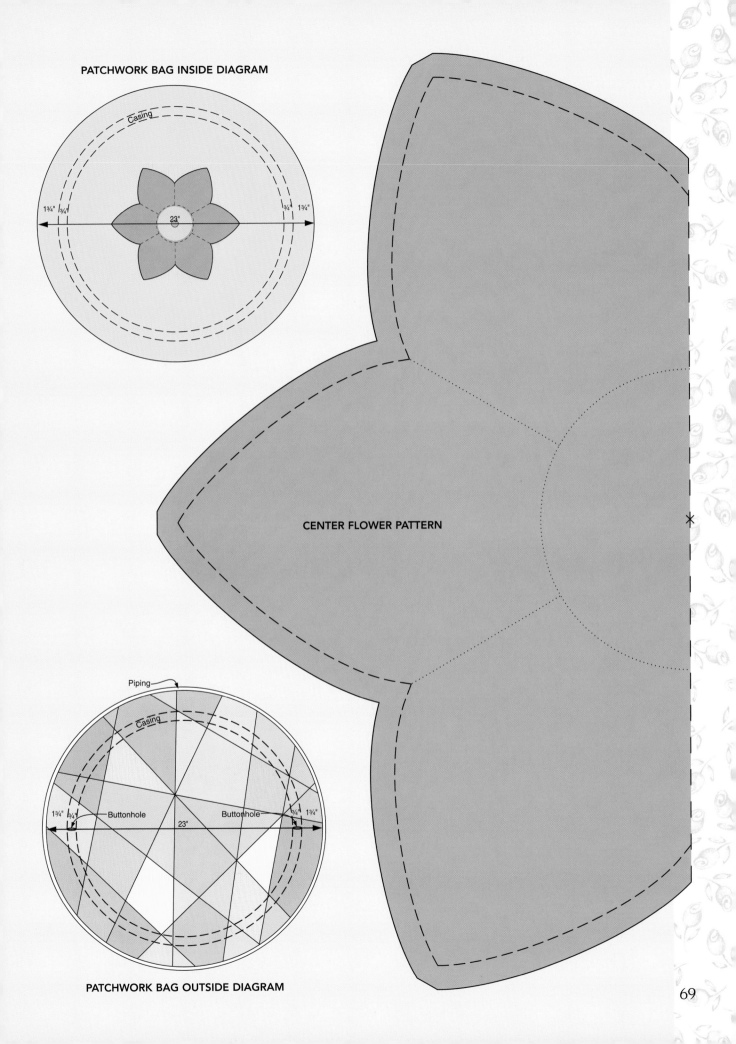

PATCHWORK BAG INSIDE DIAGRAM

Casing

1¾" ¾" 23" ¾" 1¾"

CENTER FLOWER PATTERN

Piping

Casing

1¾" ¾" Buttonhole 23" Buttonhole ¾" 1¾"

PATCHWORK BAG OUTSIDE DIAGRAM

special touches

ring life to your living spaces
by adding special touches
you can make yourself. Create an
heirloom-quality cross-stitch sampler,
stencil a vintage-looking lampshade,
and paint striking drawer pulls; all this
and more await you in this fun-filled
chapter of home accessories.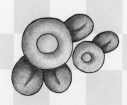

sentimental sampler

This cross-stitch sampler quotes words of wisdom to be treasured through the generations.

WHAT YOU'LL NEED

18x16-inch piece of 18-count light yellow Ariosa fabric
Cotton embroidery floss as listed in key
Needle
Desired mat and frame

HERE'S HOW

1 Tape or zigzag the edges of the Ariosa fabric to prevent fraying. Find the center of the chart, *pages 74–75*, and the center of the fabric. Begin stitching there. Use three plies of floss to work all cross-stitches over two threads of fabric.

2 Use the diagrams, *page 192*, to work the specialty stitches. Use the number of plies for each specialty stitch indicated in key.

3 Press finished stitchery from the back. Mat and frame sampler as desired.

Anchor		DMC
002	⊡	000 White
1025	♥	347 Deep salmon
217	☒	367 Pistachio
1047	◯	402 Mahogany
297	☆	444 Lemon
267	▢	470 Medium avocado
265	⊞	471 Light avocado
859	◉	523 Olive drab
090	⊟	554 Violet
324	⊠	721 Bittersweet
1021	◇	761 Light salmon
175	⋀	794 Cornflower blue
132	♡	797 Royal blue
137	◆	798 Delft blue
337	▽	922 Light copper
244	◎	987 Forest green
268	∿	3346 Hunter green
266	⊕	3347 Yellow-green
262	⊞	3363 Loden
306	●	3820 Straw
028	⊠	3832 Medium raspberry
031	⠆	3833 Light raspberry
099	△	3835 Grape

BLENDED NEEDLE

1022	✴	352 Coral (1X) and
009		760 True salmon (2X)
255	▮	907 Parrot green (2X) and
279		3819 Moss green (1X)
297	▢	444 Lemon (1X) and
305		725 Topaz (1X) and
303		742 Tangerine (1X)

HALF CROSS-STITCH
(stitch in direction of symbol)

| 386 | ◪ | 3823 Yellow – tulip border (2X) |

BLENDED-NEEDLE HALF CROSS-STITCH
(stitch in direction of symbol)

| 305 | ◪ | 725 Topaz (1X) and |
| 303 | | 742 Tangerine (1X) – border and center shadow |

BACKSTITCH

403	╱	310 Black – lace edging (2X)
1025	╱	347 Deep salmon – lettering (3X)
217	╱	367 Pistachio – stem and leaves for flowers on sides (3X)
265	╱	471 Light avocado – leaves for small flowers (2X)
338	╱	921 True copper – area around lettering (3X)
337	╱	922 Light copper – small flower centers (2X)
355	╱	975 Golden brown – border (2X)
1041	╱	844 Beaver gray – all other stitches (2X)

BLENDED-NEEDLE BACKSTITCH

| 009 | ╱ | 352 Coral (1X) and |
| 1022 | | 760 True salmon (1X) – tulips |

STRAIGHT STITCH

| 338 | ╱ | 921 True copper – area around lettering (3X) |

LARGE CROSS-STITCH

| 1041 | ✕ | 844 Beaver gray – border (2X) |

LAZY DAISY

| 858 | ⬭ | 3052 Gray-green – tulip border (3X) |

RUNNING STITCH WITH BOW

| 897 | ╱ | 221 Shell pink – area around lettering (2X) |

FRENCH KNOT

403	●	310 Black – lace edging
1025	●	347 Deep salmon – flowers around lettering (3X wrapped once)
1041	●	844 Beaver gray – border (3X wrapped once)
337	●	922 Light copper – background (4X wrapped twice)

Stitch count: *179 high x 147 wide*
Finished design sizes:
18-count fabric – 19⅞ x 16⅓ inches
16-count fabric – 22⅜ x 18⅜ inches
14-count fabric – 25½ x 21 inches

TO THINE OWN SELF CROSS-STITCH PATTERN/TOP LEFT

TO THINE OWN SELF CROSS-STITCH PATTERN/TOP RIGHT

TO THINE OWN SELF CROSS-STITCH PATTERN/BOTTOM LEFT

TO THINE OWN SELF CROSS-STITCH PATTERN/BOTTOM RIGHT

pretty-as-a-posy frame

Ready to show off any keepsake photograph or drawing, this vivid frame is created from colorful sculpted clay.

WHAT YOU'LL NEED

Flat picture frame in
  desired size
Yellow mat to fit frame
  (available at framing shops)
Oven-bakeable clay, such as
  Sculpey, in pink, lavender,
  blue, orange, yellow, red,
  and green
Small sharp knife
Oven baking dish
Acrylic paints in white, red, and
  deep yellow
Heavy paper
Decorative-edge scissors
Pencil
Light blue fine-point paint pen

HERE'S HOW

1 Create the flowers using clay. *To make pink roses*, roll out a piece of clay into a roll about 2½ inches long and ⅛ inch thick. Coil it into a rose shape.

2 *To make blue flowers*, roll a smooth round ball to about the size of a large raisin. Gently flatten it. Roll a smaller yellow ball for the center, and press it into the blue flower.

3 *To make lavender flowers*, roll 6 small balls about ⅛ inch in diameter and arrange in a circle. Press together. Shape several small white balls and press into the center. Roll a red ball and press into the center.

4 *To make orange flowers*, roll pea-size clay balls. Add a tiny yellow ball for the center dot and flatten.

5 *To make small green leaves*, shape small oblong ovals. Flatten them slightly. Pinch the ends to a point. Make a crease by pressing a knife blade at an angle down the center.

6 *To make chubby rounded leaves*, roll a piece of clay about ½ inch long and ³⁄₁₆ inch thick. Fold in half.

7 Bake all flowers in oven baking dish according to the manufacturer's instructions. Let cool.

8 Paint the frame white if needed. Let dry. Using a tiny brush and red acrylic paint, paint small red checks on the frame.

9 To make the light blue lacy line, cut strips of heavy paper using decorative-edge scissors.

Lay down the strips around the edge, measuring and taping in place. Trace lightly around the paper pattern, and remove it. Draw over the pencil line with a light blue fine-point paint pen. Add small blue flowers.

10 Place mat into frame without glass. Glue the clay flowers onto the corners of the mat as shown. It is important to have the mat in place in the frame to avoid gluing the flowers where the frame overlaps the mat.

11 To make small yellow dots on the mat, dip the handle of a paintbrush in paint and dot the mat board surface. Let dry.

vintage-look shade

So easy to stencil, this patterned lampshade looks great in a variety of hues to coordinate with your personal color schemes.

WHAT YOU'LL NEED

Permanent fine-line marker
Two 3×3-inch pieces of acetate
Crafts knife
Disposable foam plate
Acrylic paints in olive and
  orange or other desired colors
Stenciling brush
Purchased lampshade
Masking tape
Thick white crafts glue
Dark olive fringe in length to fit
  around bottom of lampshade
Olive braid in lengths to fit
  around top and bottom of
  lampshade

HERE'S HOW

1 Trace flower and leaf patterns, *below*, onto two small pieces of acetate with a permanent marker. Use a crafts knife to remove the inside shapes.

2 Place a small amount of orange paint onto a foam plate. Place the flower stencil on the lampshade and tape in place. Dip the stenciling brush into the paint and dab off. Holding the stencil firmly in place, tap the brush in the openings of the flower stencil. When all areas are lightly covered with paint, move the stencil to another area and repeat, being careful not to work too closely to the wet paint. Continue stenciling flowers around the lampshade, rotating the pattern and leaving room for the leaves. Let the paint dry.

3 Create the leaves in the same manner as the flowers, using olive paint. Stencil one or two leaves near every flower. Let dry.

4 Glue fringe around the bottom edge of the lampshade. Trim any excess fringe. Glue braid over the top of the fringe and around the top rim. Let the glue dry.

**LAMPSHADE LEAF AND
FLOWER STENCIL PATTERNS**

bowlies candleholder

Create a lighthearted glow by setting a candle in a stack of fun-loving wood bowls.

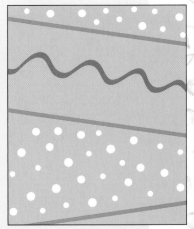

WHAT YOU'LL NEED
4 wood bowls; white spray primer
Medium flat and fine liner paintbrushes
Acrylic paints in dark green, light green, pink, yellow, lime green, black, lavender, sky blue, white, and medium blue
Jumbo and regular pencils with round erasers
Black fine-line marker; toothpick
Clear gloss spray varnish
Pillar candle; candies, optional

HERE'S HOW
1 Wash and dry the bowls. Spray a light coat of white spray primer on each bowl. Let dry.

2 *For the green bowl,* paint the inside dark green. Paint the outside a lighter green. Let dry. Using a pencil, draw a line around rim about ¼ inch from the edge. Add scallops around the edge, using the pattern, *below,* as a guide. Use a medium flat brush to paint the scallops pink and yellow. Use a fine liner brush to paint the outlines. Add yellow and green dots by dipping the handle of a paintbrush in paint and dotting onto surface. Let dry.

3 *For the lavender bowl,* paint the inside pink. Paint the outside lavender. Let dry. To paint red flowers as shown, *below,* dip the eraser of a jumbo pencil into paint and dot onto surface. Let dry. To make blue flowers, dip the handle end of a paintbrush into paint, and dot in a circle, making six petals. Let dry. Make yellow flower centers and white dots using a paintbrush handle. Add lime green leaves using a fine liner brush. Outline the flowers and leaves using a black marker.

4 *For the yellow bowl,* paint the inside orange. Paint the outside yellow. Let dry. Make red flowers, *below,* by dipping the eraser of a pencil into paint and dotting onto surface. Let dry. Add lime green oval leaves using a fine liner brush. Use the handle of a paintbrush to make yellow flower centers and black dots between flowers.

5 *For the blue bowl,* paint the inside medium blue. Paint the outside sky blue. Let dry. Using a fine liner brush, paint stripes in medium blue, wavy lines in pink, and add tiny white dots with a toothpick, using the pattern, *below,* as a guide. Let the paint dry.

6 Spray bowls with two light coats of varnish. Let dry. Stack bowls, and place a candle in top. Fill top bowl with candies, if desired.

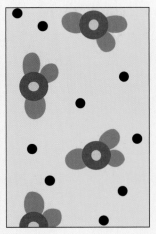
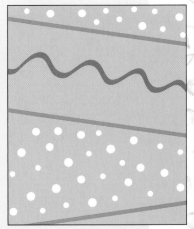

BOWL DESIGN PATTERNS

HOUSE
HOT PAD

happy-cook hot pads

Spending time in the kitchen is a pleasure with these hot pads at hand. The patterns are on pages 87–89.

WHAT YOU'LL NEED

For the House hot pad:
6×6-inch piece of yellow fabric
6×8-inch piece of red fabric
Scrap of blue fabric for door
Scrap of brown fabric for windows
Scrap of gray fabric for panes
Scrap of light brown fabric for chimney
Scrap of gold print fabric for chimney cap
Scrap of green fabrics for leaves and shutters
Scrap of purple fabric for flowers
Scrap of orange fabric for sun

For the Floral hot pad:
6×6-inch piece of green fabric for leaves and stem
Scrap of contrasting green fabric for leaves
Scraps of purple, blue, red, and orange fabrics for flowers

For the Home hot pad:
8×8-inch piece of gold print fabric for letters
Scraps of 2 shades of green fabric for leaves
Scraps of purple and blue fabrics
1¼-inch shank heart button

For all hot pads:
Paperbacked fusible webbing
¼ yard of black fabric for background
Embroidery floss
Fleece
½ yard of black-and-white checked fabric for backing and binding
#5 black pearl cotton or black spray paint, if desired
Matching threads
1-inch-diameter cabone ring
Crochet hook
¼-inch-wide small red grosgrain bow

HOME
HOT PAD

FLORAL
HOT PAD

continued on page 86

happy-cook hot pads — *continued*

HERE'S HOW

1 Trace the desired full-size pattern pieces, *pages 87–89*, onto paperbacked fusible webbing. Fuse the pieces to the corresponding fabrics. Cut out the fabric pieces and fuse to 7×7½-inch black background using the pattern as a guide. Machine-satin-stitch in matching thread or embroider according to the stitching diagrams and patterns, *pages 86–89*.

2 Layer the appliquéd piece, fleece, and backing fabric. Quilt through all layers as desired.

3 To make the binding, cut a 36×1¼-inch strip from checked fabric. Press in half lengthwise. Turn raw edges to inside and press, leaving a ⅜-inch binding. Bind the raw edges of the hot pad. Trim excess, leaving ¼ inch to turn under at the end.

4 Single-crochet around the cabone ring with black pearl cotton or spray-paint it black, if desired. Stitch the ring to the top left corner of the hot pad. Add a small red ribbon bow to the corner.

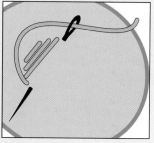

SATIN STITCH

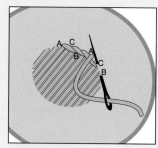

STEM STITCH

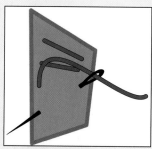

STRAIGHT STITCH

FLORAL HOT PAD PATTERN

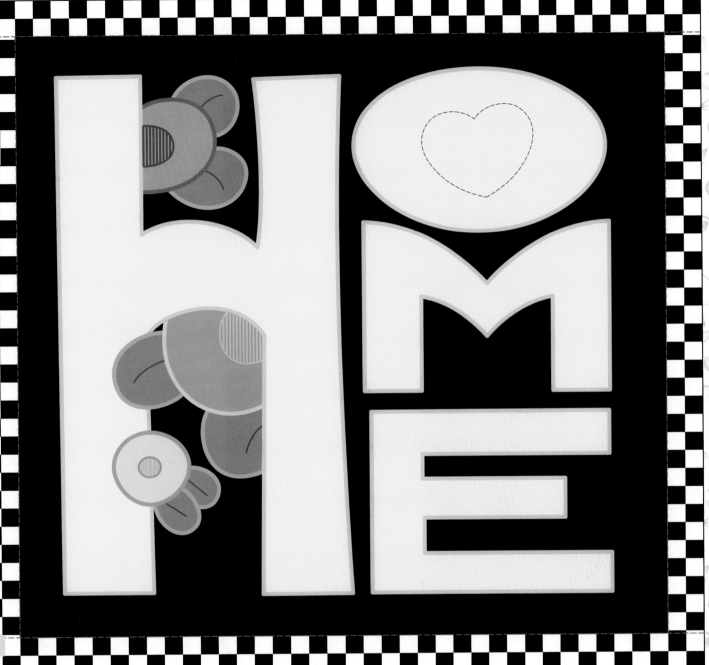

HOME HOT PAD PATTERN

dainty drawer pulls

Inexpensive wood knobs become engaging works of art when painted with bold floral designs. Paint several the same or vary designs to suit your style.

WHAT YOU'LL NEED
Unfinished wood knobs
Fine sandpaper
Tack cloth
Tracing paper
Pencil
Acrylic paints in black, red, light
  blue, lime green, green,
  brown, white, and yellow
Fine liner paintbrush
Toothpick
Acrylic gloss varnish

HERE'S HOW

1 Lightly sand the knobs. Wipe with a tack cloth.

2 Trace the desired patterns at *right*. Draw over the back of the pattern with a soft pencil. Center the pattern, pencil side down, on the wood knob. Trace the pattern lines onto the top of the knob.

3 Using the original pattern as a color guide, paint the knob. Start with the flower and leaves. Let the paint dry.

4 Add the black details and white highlights on the leaves and flowers using a fine liner paintbrush. Let the paint dry.

5 Paint the solid black background, touching up leaves and flowers as necessary. Paint the underside of the knob. Let the paint dry.

6 To add the small white dots on the black background, dip the handle of a paintbrush into white paint and dot onto the surface. For the black and white dots in the sunflower center, use a toothpick in the same manner. Let the paint dry.

7 Apply a light coat of varnish over the entire knob. Let dry. Apply a second coat. Let dry.

DRAWER PULL PATTERNS

91

prettied-up porches & patios

hen guests see your prettied-up porches and patios, they'll know their visit is welcome. No matter what kind of entry your home has, brighten it up with projects inspired by Mary's illustrations filled with warmth and charm.

BE GOOD FOR SOMETHING

SIMPLE

PLEASURES

everlasting flowers

Give the phrase "rock garden" new meaning when you line your walkway with rocks painted and arranged like Mary's vibrant flowers.

WHAT YOU'LL NEED

Smooth, flat river rocks (available at garden centers)
Medium flat paintbrush
Acrylic outdoor paints in purple, lavender, blue, sky blue, white, yellow, red, pink, green, and lime green

HERE'S HOW

1 Gather or purchase flat rocks. Choose rocks with round, oval, oblong, and triangular shapes. Wash and dry the rocks.

2 Using the photograph, *opposite*, for inspiration, paint rocks solid colors first. Let the paint dry.

3 For highlights, use a lime green over the green, light blue over blue, lavender over purple, and pink over red. Apply a small amount of paint to the center or around the area you want to highlight. The base coat should not be completely covered. Let dry. For the 5-petal blue flowers, add white to the inside points. Let dry.

4 Arrange the rocks in flower configurations in the garden, on sidewalks, on porch steps, or wherever everlasting flowers might brighten the way.

adorable address plate

Your house will stand out on the block with this charming plate announcing your street number.

WHAT YOU'LL NEED
Wood plaque in desired size and shape
Sandpaper; tack cloth
White spray primer
Acrylic paints in peach, white, black, yellow, red, green, and light blue
Medium and small flat paintbrushes
Tracing paper and pencil
Scissors
¼-inch-thick wood for numbers
Jigsaw
White pencil
Wood glue
Clear gloss, non-yellowing outdoor varnish
Hanger for back

HERE'S HOW

1 Sand the wood plaque. Remove dust with a tack cloth. Prime with white spray primer in a well-ventilated work area. Let the paint dry.

2 Paint the outer edge peach as shown. Paint black and white checks around the inside border. Paint top surface black. Let the paint dry.

3 Trace the numbers you need from the full-size patterns on *page 99*. Cut out and trace onto ¼-inch-thick wood. Cut out the numbers with a jigsaw, and sand the edges. Remove dust with a tack cloth.

4 Paint the numbers white. Let dry. Paint a second coat and let dry.

5 Center and place numbers onto the plaque, leaving room for the flower designs.

6 Trace the full-size floral pattern, *page 98*, onto tracing paper, cut out, and place on plaque. Trace around the flower pattern. Reverse the pattern for the right side. You may need to use a white pencil. Remove numbers. Paint flowers using the pattern as a guide. Let dry. Outline the flowers with a fine liner paintbrush. Let dry.

7 Using wood glue, affix numbers onto the plaque. Let glue dry.

8 Seal all surfaces of the plaque with a clear, non-yellowing gloss varnish. Let dry. Attach a hook on the back for hanging.

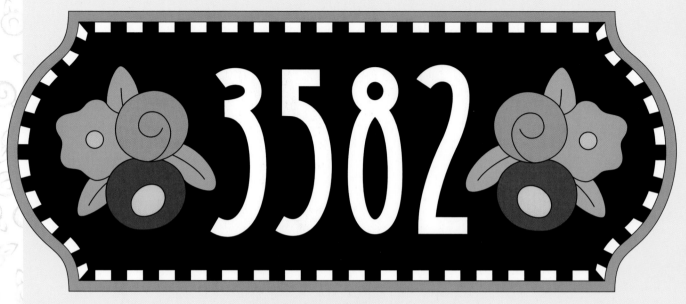

ADDRESS PLATE PLACEMENT DIAGRAM

ADDRESS PLATE FLOWER PATTERN

1 2 3 4 5
6 7 8 9 0

ADDRESS PLATE NUMBER PATTERNS

finial plant pokes

Let your imagination be your guide when painting these playful plant decorations.

WHAT YOU'LL NEED
Wood finials in desired shapes
Drill and ¼- and ¹⁄₁₆-inch bits
Round toothpick
Thick white crafts glue
White spray primer
Acrylic paints in white, red, yellow, blue, green, and black
Medium flat and fine liner paintbrushes
Pencil with round eraser
Clear gloss varnish

HERE'S HOW
1 Drill a ¼-inch hole in the center of each finial as shown in the photograph, *opposite*, each approximately ½ inch deep. Cut a small piece of round toothpick for each perch. Drill a ¹⁄₁₆-inch hole just below the ¼-inch hole for the perch. Glue the toothpick in place. Let the glue dry.

2 In a well-ventilated work area, prime the finials with white spray primer. Let dry.

3 Paint the birdhouses as shown, using the patterns *below* as guides. Paint the large background areas first. Let dry. Paint in the smaller areas, such as the rings around the finials. Let the paint dry.

4 Add small details. *To make thin lines,* use a fine liner paintbrush. *To make dots and round flowers,* dip the handle of a paintbrush into paint, and dot the surface. *To make larger dots,* like the white dots on the red roof, dip a round pencil eraser into paint and carefully dot the surface. Let dry.

5 Coat the entire surface with a coat of clear gloss varnish. Let dry.

RED/WHITE PLANT POKE PATTERNS

BLUE/WHITE PLANT POKE PATTERN

so-sweet footstool

Rest your teacup or put up your feet on this pretty painted footstool which is just the right size for your porch or patio. The patterns are on pages 104–105.

WHAT YOU'LL NEED
Fine sandpaper
Small purchased wooden
  footstool approximately
  7¼×12 inches
Tack cloth
White spray primer; paintbrushes
Acrylic paints in cream, green,
  burnt orange, and red
Tracing paper; pencil; ruler
Clear gloss spray varnish

HERE'S HOW

1 Sand all surfaces of the footstool. Wipe off the dust using a tack cloth.

2 Paint the footstool with white spray primer. Let the primer dry.

3 Paint stool with cream acrylic paint. Let the paint dry.

4 Trace the patterns, *pages 104–105*, onto tracing paper. Cut out the designs for the center top and transfer them to the footstool using the placement diagram on *page 104*. Adjust the patterns to fit thje footstool size if necessary.

5 If the border size does not match the measurements of your footstool, use a ruler to mark the center of each footstool edge.

6 Align the center of the scallop border pattern with the center mark on the edge of the footstool. Trace around the scallop border on all edges of the footstool.

7 Transfer the scallop and heart patterns to the sides of the footstool.

8 Paint the designs as shown on patterns using red, green, and burnt orange paints. Let dry.

9 To paint the checks along the edges of the legs, use a ruler to draw pencil lines indicating even checks. Paint every other square red. Let the paint dry.

10 Spray the bench with one or two coats of clear gloss varnish, allowing to dry between coats.

SO-SWEET FOOTSTOOL SIDE PATTERN

SO-SWEET FOOTSTOOL PLACEMENT DIAGRAM

Center

SO-SWEET FOOTSTOOL TOP PATTERN

clever caddy

WHAT YOU'LL NEED

Tracing paper; #2 pencil; scissors
½-inch-thick pine; jigsaw
Tilt-blade table saw
100-grit sandpaper; tack cloth
1½-inch finishing nails
Acrylic paints in yellow, red, olive
  green, white, and dark green
Disposable foam or paper plate
Matte decoupage medium
Fine liner and medium round
  paintbrushes; tape
Clear spray varnish or sealer

HERE'S HOW

1 Use patterns and assembly
diagram, *pages 108–109*, to
measure and outline necessary
pieces on pine. Cut out pieces,
using tilt-blade table saw to cut
angles. Sand edges and remove
dust with a tack cloth.

2 Assemble the pieces as shown
in the assembly diagram on
page 108. Nail together using
1½-inch finishing nails.

3 Paint the inside of the caddy
yellow. Let dry. To make red
dots, dip the handle of a small
paintbrush in red paint and dot
onto the surface. Let dry.

4 On a disposable plate, mix
3 tablespoons of decoupage
medium and a teaspoon of dark
green paint. This will make the
paint translucent. Paint mix onto
exterior and center handle in the
same direction as the wood
grain, keeping the flow of paint
even, especially around the
edges. If you want a more
intense color, apply a second
coat. This will make the paint
less transparent.

5 Trace the flower pattern,
page 109, onto tracing
paper. Using a #2 pencil,
color the back of pattern.
Tape pattern on box.

continued on page 108

This easy-to-construct, portable
storage tote keeps you organized
in style.

clever caddy — *continued*

Draw over lines with a sharp pencil. Paint design using red, yellow, and dark green. Let dry.

6 Using 100-grit sandpaper, sand off paint from edges for a worn look. Remove dust with a tack cloth.

7 Apply a coat of clear varnish to the entire piece. Let dry.

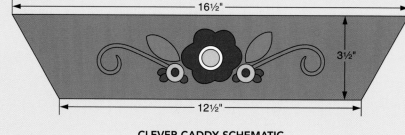

CLEVER CADDY SCHEMATIC

16½"
3½"
12½"

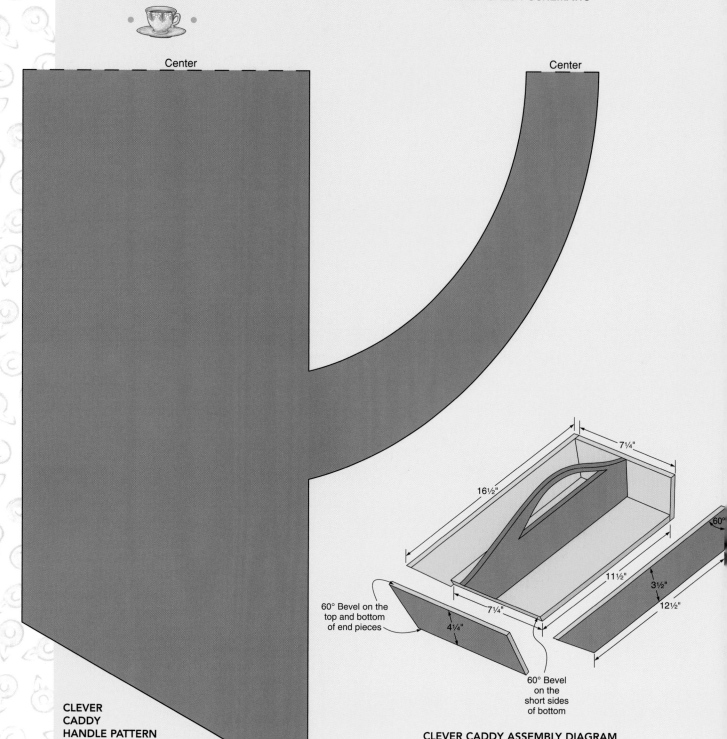

Center

Center

CLEVER CADDY HANDLE PATTERN

CLEVER CADDY ASSEMBLY DIAGRAM

7¼"
16½"
11½"
3½"
12½"
7¼"
4¼"

60° Bevel on the top and bottom of end pieces

60° Bevel on the short sides of bottom

60°

**CLEVER
CADDY SIDE
PATTERN**

CLEVER CADDY END—SIDE VIEW

CLEVER CADDY BOTTOM—SIDE VIEW

Center

**CLEVER
CADDY FLOWER
PATTERN**

screen door decor

Made from a sheet of magnetic vinyl, these striking black-and-white designs add interest to your screen door.

WHAT YOU'LL NEED
Tracing paper and pencil
Sharp scissors
White magnetic vinyl
 (available in arts and crafts
 stores and in home centers by
 air-vent register covers)
Broad-tip permanent black
 marker
Pierced earring posts and backs
Hot-glue gun and hot-glue sticks

HERE'S HOW

1 Trace the full-size patterns, *pages 112–113,* onto tracing paper. Cut out and trace onto white magnetic vinyl.

2 For detail lines, use a sharp #2 pencil to color the back side of pattern. Place pattern on vinyl, right side up. Trace around edge and detail lines, pressing firmly to transfer the lines.

3 Cut out the shapes with sharp scissors. Outline edges, detail lines, and solid areas using a broad-tip black permanent marker. Let dry.

4 Wipe off any remaining pencil lines with a wet cloth. Glue three or four earring posts to the back side of each design and let dry. Decide the arrangement of the flowers. Push the earring posts through the screen, using earring backs to secure each piece on the other side.

SCREEN DOOR DECOR
FLOWER PATTERNS

**SCREEN DOOR DECOR
FLOWER PATTERNS**

come to the garden

nexpected creations and enticing bursts of color beckon you to come to the garden. Join us as we use Mary's designs to craft clever accessories and lovely decorations to make the most of your favorite planting spot.

SOW GOOD SERVICES; SWEET REMEMBRANCES WILL GROW FROM THEM.
Mde. de Stael

Just for you!

FRIENDS ARE THE FLOWERS IN THE GARDEN OF LIFE.

garden treasures

Fill your garden with love by adding these heart-shape crafts to your collection.

WHAT YOU'LL NEED

Wood hearts (2 per stem)
Wood glue
Wood leaves (4 per stem) or
 ½-inch pine, tracing paper,
 pencil, scissors, and jigsaw
Wood skewer or dowel
 approximately ⅛-inch thick
Drill and bit to match skewer
 width and wire
Medium flat paintbrush
Acrylic paints in lime green,
 dark green, red, peach, pink,
 and yellow
Wood beads
Green floral wire
Wire cutters
Clear varnish

HERE'S HOW

1 Prepare the wooden hearts and leaves first. Glue two ¼-inch thick wood hearts back-to-back with wood glue or purchase one wood heart that is ½-inch thick. If not using purchased leaves, trace the leaf pattern, *below*, and transfer to pine. Cut out four with a jigsaw.

2 To make the stem, use a wooden skewer or a dowel. Drill a hole into the heart using a bit to match the width of the skewer. Drill the hole from the center top to the bottom.

3 Paint the wood pieces before assembling. Paint the skewer dark green. Paint the beads yellow. *To paint the dark-colored heart,* paint the heart red first. Let dry. Put a dab of peach paint on brush. Begin to brush onto one corner, brushing downward and fading out into the red. Add more layers of peach until you are satisfied with the color. *To paint the light heart,* paint entire heart peach. Let dry. Apply a dab of light pink paint on brush, and paint in the same manner as the dark colored heart.

4 *To paint leaves,* paint dark green first. Let dry. Highlight with lime green. Using a dab of lime green paint, begin painting on one side or end. Brush out into dark green. Let dry.

5 Insert stem into heart and secure with glue. Use green floral wire to attach the leaves and yellow beads. Drill holes into the leaves the same thickness as the wire. Insert three 3-inch pieces of wire into top of hearts. Attach beads and reinforce with glue. Wrap a piece of wire around stem, and insert into leaves. Add a dab of glue. Let dry. Spray with clear varnish. Let dry.

LEAF PATTERN

hobby hat

Any garden lover will have it made in the shade with this straw hat enhanced with felt flowers.

WHAT YOU'LL NEED
36-inch piece of wide black
  grosgrain ribbon
Straw hat with brim
Hot-glue gun and glue sticks
Scissors
Tracing paper
Pencil
Pink felt
Needle
Pink thread
Yellow pom-poms
Black chenille stems
Green silk leaves

HERE'S HOW

1 Wrap the length of ribbon around the base of the crown of the hat, and glue in place, leaving tails. Fold the ribbons in half lengthwise, and clip the ends diagonally.

2 To make flowers, enlarge and trace the pattern, *right*, onto tracing paper, and cut out. Trace onto pink felt, and cut out.

3 Fold the felt piece in half lengthwise. Use a running stitch to sew the long open sides together. Pull tightly to gather felt. Sew several tight stitches at the end to hold the gathers in place.

4 Coil the gathered fabric into a flower shape with the narrow end in the center. Sew several stitches to hold the coil in place. Sew a small yellow pom-pom in the center.

5 Cut three 6-inch pieces of black chenille stem. Insert one end of chenille stem under yellow ball and out the other side. Repeat with the remaining two chenille stems to make six stamens. Curl the ends.

6 Glue green silk leaves to flowers where desired.

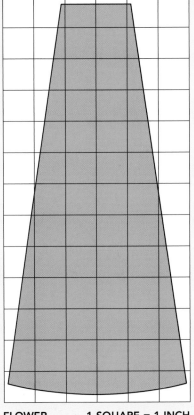

FLOWER PATTERN   **1 SQUARE = 1 INCH**

HOW GOOD SERVICES; SWEET REMEMBRANCES WILL GROW FROM THEM. *Mde. de Staël*

A kind reminder and a lovely addition to any garden, this painted brick is a favorite beacon for the garden.

WHAT YOU'LL NEED

Smooth patio brick approximately 7½×15¼ inches
White spray primer
Photocopy or tracing paper
Scissors
#2 pencil; ruler
Tape
Flat medium and fine liner paintbrushes
Acrylic paints in baby blue, white, light yellow, light lime green, red, orange, and pink
Fine-line, black permanent marker

HERE'S HOW

1 Wash the brick. Let it dry. Spray brick with white primer. Let it dry.

2 Using a pencil and ruler, draw the border about ¾ inch around the edge. Trace the full-size patterns, *pages 122–123*, onto tracing paper or photocopy the pattern. Adjust the pattern to fit if necessary. Trim pattern close to words. Use a #2 or soft pencil to color the back of the pattern. Center the pattern on the brick. Tape it firmly in place. Use a sharp pencil or pen to draw over outline of each letter, transferring the pattern onto the brick.

3 Paint a baby blue background inside the border. Let it dry. Using a small amount of white on a brush, lightly stroke the blue area to create a mottled look. Do not completely cover the blue.

4 Paint the outside border light yellow. Let it dry.

5 Using a small round brush, paint the inside of the letters red. Let dry. Paint over top half of letters with orange fading into the red to create a shaded look. Paint the flower as shown on the pattern. Let the paint dry.

6 Use a black marker to outline the letters, border, and flowers.

STEPPING STONE FULL-SIZE PATTERN

SERVICES;

EMBRANCES

FROM THEM.

A fence or garden gate
offers a cheerful display
whether or not the flowers
are in bloom.

124

vivid climbing vine

WHAT YOU'LL NEED

Tracing paper, pencil; scissors
½- or ¾-inch-thick smooth
  green treated cedar
Sandpaper; white spray primer
Graphite paper, optional
Medium flat paint brush; water
Acrylic paints in grass green,
  lime green, red, dark pink,
  orange-yellow, bright yellow,
  blue, pastel blue, purple,
  lavender, white, and pastel
  gray-blue
Medium-point black paint marker
Spray varnish
¼-inch-thick vinyl-coated
  electrical wiring (available at
  hardware stores and home
  centers)
Heavy-duty staple gun

HERE'S HOW

1 Trace the full-size patterns,
pages 126–129, onto
tracing paper. Cut out and trace
onto a piece of cedar. Cut out.
Sand rough edges.

2 Prime the flowers on both
sides with white spray
primer. Let dry.

3 Transfer the inner pencil
lines onto flower. You may
use graphite paper or rub a
pencil heavily onto the backside
of tracing paper. Lay the paper
onto the flower, and retrace
patterns, transferring outline to
the primed surface.

4 Paint the flowers and leaves
with the base colors first. To
highlight the base colors, use a
very small amount of paint on a
medium-size flat brush. This
should be an almost dry brush.
Brush over the areas you want
to lighten. Paint leaves grass
green. Highlight with lime
green. Highlight the red
flower with pink. Paint the
white daisy pastel gray-blue and
highlight with white. Highlight
the purple flower with lavender.
Highlight the blue flower with a
lighter blue. Let the paint dry.
Paint the flower centers orange-
yellow and highlight with bright
yellow. Let dry. Add more thin
layers of light-colored paint until
the desired color is achieved.

5 When all the paint is dry,
outline areas with a black
paint marker as shown.

6 Spray two or three coats of
varnish on wood flowers.
Let dry between coats.

7 Cut a piece of vinyl-coated
electrical wiring to the
desired length for the vine.
Paint it green, and let it dry.
Paint a second coat, if needed.
Spray with varnish and let dry.

8 Use a heavy-duty staple gun
to attach the vinyl wire to
the back of the flowers. To
display, wind the vine around a
fence or gate.

BLUE FLOWER PATTERN

PURPLE FLOWER PATTERN

RED FLOWER PATTERN

WHITE FLOWER PATTERN

129

antern luminarias

These fun luminarias add charm by day and a soft glow at night, whether there is just one or a merry dozen.

WHAT YOU'LL NEED
Metal shepherd's hook (available in the garden department of a hardware store or home center)
White spray primer
Acrylic paints in dark green, grass green, lime green, red, yellow, blue, black, white, and purple
Medium flat and fine liner paintbrushes; wire cutters
¼-inch vinyl-coated wire (available at hardware store or home center); clear spray varnish
Tracing paper; pencil; scissors
¼-inch-thick cedar wood
Drill and ¼-inch drill bit
Round ¾-inch wood bead
Disk-shape wood bead
Yellow plastic lacing
Small pieces of crafting aluminum
Strong adhesive, such as E6000
Small sharp knife; 18-gauge wire
Lantern (available at gift stores)

HERE'S HOW

1 Spray the shepherd's hook with primer. Paint hook dark green. Let dry. Apply another coat, if needed.

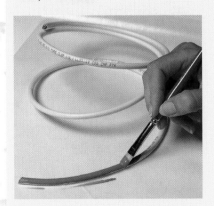

2 Prepare vine. Cut a length of vinyl-coated wire as long as desired. Paint wire lime green. Let it dry. Apply a second coat of paint. Let dry. Spray a coat of clear varnish over wire. Let dry.

3 Beginning at the base, wind the vine around the hook, coiling around a couple times to anchor it. Then curve it outward to hold the wooden heart. Spray the hook and wire with two more coats of varnish.

4 Trace the full-size heart pattern, *page 133,* onto tracing paper. Cut out the pattern and trace it onto a piece of cedar. Cut out heart and sand rough edges. Drill a hole from top center down to the bottom.

5 Paint the heart red. While paint is still wet, blend in a small dab of yellow paint on the front of the heart, working out from the center and leaving the outer edges a brighter red. Add more yellow in the center until you are satisfied with the blend of color. Let dry.

6 Using fine liner brush, add crisscrossed lines in black. To make black dots where lines intersect, use the handle of a paintbrush.

7 Add yellow dots in center of diamond shapes. Let dry.

8 Enlarge the holes in beads if needed, using the same drill bit as on the heart. Paint the round bead yellow. Let dry. Paint the disk bead blue. Let dry. Add blue dots to the yellow bead. Let dry.

9 To make the yellow tassel, wrap plastic lacing around four fingers about 16 times. Tie loops tightly with another piece of plastic lacing about 12 inches long. Clip the bottom of loops to make a tassel. Pull tie ends first through blue bead, then yellow bead, and then heart. The head of tassel should be snugly stuck into the bead holes. Holding the heart and tassel firmly by the tie ends, insert the vine end into the hole, fitting snugly. Add a dab of adhesive into the hole, if needed.

continued on page 132

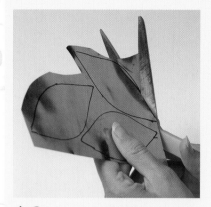

10 To make leaves, trace the full-size pattern, *opposite*, onto thin crafting aluminum and cut out.

11 Run a pen or pencil down the center of the leaf, making a crease. Slightly bend at the crease to make it look more like a real leaf.

12 Cut a piece of 18-gauge wire about 4 inches long. Lay the wire on the back side of leaf along the crease. Spread a generous amount of adhesive to attach the wire, leaving a stem off one end. Let dry. Make three or more leaves.

13 Spray the leaves with white spray primer. Let dry. Paint two coats of dark green paint onto both sides of leaves, allowing to dry between coats. Apply a small amount of lime green paint onto brush and paint the leaves by stroking from the outer edge inward. Allow the dark green to show through in the creased areas. Let dry

14 With a small, sharp knife, pierce small holes into vinyl-coated wire where you want to insert leaves. Insert the stems of leaves into the holes, securing with glue if needed.

15 Paint an array of flowers on the lantern, using the patterns, *opposite*, as guides. Then add small oval leaves using grass green and lime green paints. *To make the round flowers,* dip a round pencil eraser or a dowel into paint and dot onto surface. Use the handle of a paintbrush to make the smaller center dots. *To make the blue flowers,* make a series of about six dots in a circle and paint the center white with a fine liner brush. Add a yellow dot in center. *To make the purple flowers,* use a small flat brush to paint an X; then add a third line crossing the X to complete the flower shape. Paint the darker center using a fine liner brush. Add a yellow center. *To paint the white daisies,* paint a circle of white dots with a little space between each. With a small brush, pull the paint from dots to the center. Add a yellow center dot. *To paint the yellow tulips,* paint a small cup shape first; then add the three points. Let the paint dry. Spray with varnish. Let dry.

LANTERN FLOWER PATTERNS

LANTERN LEAF PATTERN

LANTERN HEART PATTERN

whimsical watering can

Sprinkling your flowers is a delight with this easy-to-decoupage can.

WHAT YOU'LL NEED
Tracing paper
Pencil
Scissors
Yellow paper
Patterned or solid memory book papers in pink, green, blue, and yellow (available in discount and crafts stores)
Newspapers
Watering can
White spray primer
Disposable foam or paper plate
Acrylic paints in light gray-blue and white
Small sea sponge
Black-and-white checked paper
Tape measure
Decoupage medium
Fine-point black paint pen

HERE'S HOW

1 Trace the full-size patterns, *page 137,* onto tracing paper and cut out. Trace the shapes onto the patterned and yellow paper. Carefully cut out the circles, leaves, and rectangles. Cut out enough pieces to cover the watering can. To cut smoother edges on the pieces, hold the scissors still and move the paper being cut. If necessary, carefully trim off any jagged edges. Be careful not to crease the pieces.

2 In a well-ventilated area, cover the work surface with newspapers. Prime the outside of the watering can with a light coat of white spray primer. Let the primer dry. Spray on a second light coat, if needed. Let it dry.

3 Cut several strips of black-and-white checked paper to fit around the watering can in the three areas as shown in the photograph, *right.* These strips should be carefully glued end-to-end so the joints will not show. Cut the correct lengths ahead of time.

4 Soak a natural sea sponge in water to soften. Squeeze out the excess water.

5 Place a small amount of white and light gray-blue paint onto a plate. Do not mix the colors.

continued on page 136

whimsical watering can — *continued*

6 Begin sponging paint onto the surface of the watering can, alternating white and blue and blending colors as desired. It is not necessary to paint the areas to be decoupaged, but paint beyond the edges so all exposed surfaces are covered.

7 Before beginning to decoupage, plan how you will arrange decoupage paper. Space the flowers according to the size of the watering can.

8 The yellow background behind the flowers is a solid piece of paper. Measure the height and width needed to fit the watering can and cut the paper to size.

9 Paint decoupage medium onto the surface of the can, position paper pieces over it, and paint more decoupage medium over the top of the pieces. Let dry.

10 When the entire can is dry, outline the flowers with a black paint pen. Let dry. Coat the entire can with another coat of decoupage medium. Let dry.

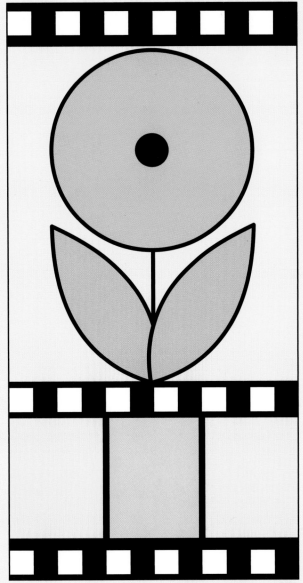

WATERING CAN PATTERN

WATERING CAN PLACEMENT

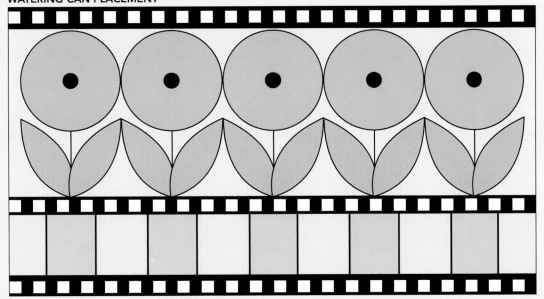

fancy flowerpots

These terra-cotta pots bloom gloriously with a combination of tiny tiles and clay flowers.

WHAT YOU'LL NEED
½-inch tiles in black and white
Terra-cotta pots
Strong adhesive, such as Liquid Nails construction adhesive
Oven-bakeable clay, such as Sculpey, in yellow, white, pink, green, red, and blue
Pencil
Crafts knife
Baking dish
Flower-shape cookie cutter

HERE'S HOW

1 Decide placement of tiles for rim of flowerpot. You can apply the tiles in a single row or in two or more rows. Glue the tiles in place. Let the adhesive dry.

2 Form the flowers and leaves from clay, using the photographs, *above and* *opposite*, as guides. *To make the round flowers,* first roll a ball for the outside color. Make an indentation in the center using a pencil. Roll a smaller ball for the flower center and press gently into the indentation. The large blue flower, *above right,* was made using a cookie cutter. *To make leaves,* press clay flat and use a crafts knife to cut out the shapes.

3 Press the flower and leaf pieces together as units and bake on a baking dish in oven according to the manufacturer's instructions. Let the pieces cool.

4 Glue the flowers onto the flowerpot as desired. Let dry.

homegrown tools

Add a "breit" touch to ordinary gardening tools by decoupaging Mary's floral designs on the handles.

WHAT YOU'LL NEED

Flower art on *page 143*
A pair of garden tools with
   wood handles
Sandpaper; tack cloth
Masking tape
Acrylic paints in yellow and
   orange-yellow
Paintbrush
Small scissors
Decoupage medium

HERE'S HOW

1 Photocopy the flower art on *page 143*. Four copies of the page will provide plenty of patterns to decoupage a pair of garden tools. Set aside.

2 Sand the tool handles until smooth. Wipe away dust using a tack cloth. Wrap a small piece of masking tape just below the handle to keep the chrome from getting painted.

4 Cut out each of the floral designs. For a smooth cut, hold the scissors still while moving the paper.

continued on page 142

3 Paint the handles yellow. Let the paint dry. Apply one or two more coats of paint until the handles are well covered, letting the paint dry between coats.

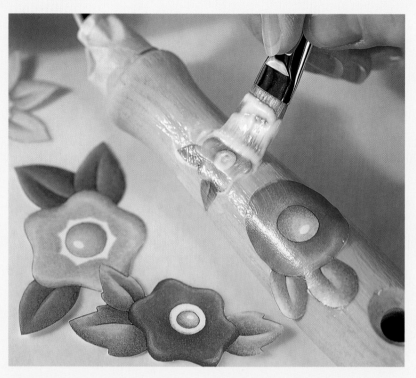

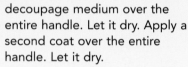

5 Paint decoupage medium on the back of each floral design before pressing it onto the tool handle.

6 Brush decoupage medium over the top of each flower as you position it on the handle. Let it dry. Apply a coat of decoupage medium over the entire handle. Let it dry. Apply a second coat over the entire handle. Let it dry.

7 To add dots, dip the handle of the paintbrush into orange-yellow paint. Dot onto surface in groups of three or four between decoupaged designs. Let the paint dry. Remove the tape from the handle.

FLOWER ART

for our nature friends

wonderful way to display your talent outdoors is by making items for our nature friends. From colorful, painted bird feeders to striking cross-stitch dog collars, each of these crafts shows your appreciation for wildlife and family pets.

HAPPY
BIRTHD[A]

A LITTLE BIRD TOLD ME.

THE GOAL of LIFE
IS LIVING IN AGREEMENT
WITH NATURE.
ZENO 335-263 B.C.

145

butterfly getaway

Even if you don't have a butterfly garden, this pretty painted house with designs inspired by Mary's illustration is sure to welcome the delicate winged friends into your yard.

WHAT YOU'LL NEED
Purchased butterfly house (available at home or garden centers)
White spray primer
Small sea sponge for painting
Disposable foam or paper plate
Acrylic paints in medium and light pink, green, black, and white
Fine and medium paintbrushes
Tracing paper
Pencil
Scissors
Clear gloss spray varnish
Pole for base

HERE'S HOW

1 Purchase a simple wooden butterfly house in a desired shape. This painted design can be adapted to almost any butterfly house.

2 In a well-ventilated work area, paint a coat of white spray primer on the house. Let it dry.

3 Place light pink and medium pink paints on plate. Don't mix paints. Soak painting sponge in water and squeeze out excess. Begin dabbing medium pink paint onto wood surface with sponge. Alternate light and medium pinks in a random pattern, sponging and blending until you have achieved the desired effect. Cover the entire base.

4 Paint the top of the roof green. Let the paint dry. Add a second coat if needed. Let dry.

5 Paint the trim areas white where checks will be. Let the paint dry. Paint a second coat, if needed, and let dry. With a pencil and ruler, draw in checks. For wide trim, first draw a line down the center. Measure and mark short lines, evenly spaced, to create squares. For narrow trim, measure off single units as wide as the trim to create squares. Using a flat paintbrush, paint in black checks. Let the paint dry.

6 Trace as many of the full-size patterns as desired from *pages 148–149*. Using a #2 or soft pencil, color the back of the tracing paper. Cut out the patterns.

7 Arrange and tape the patterns onto the butterfly house with the colored side against the wood surface. Use a sharp pencil to draw an outline around each shape.

8 Remove the patterns and paint the shapes black. Let the paint dry.

9 Wipe away any remaining pencil lines with a damp cloth. Spray two or three coats of clear gloss varnish. Let dry between coats.

10 Attach the butterfly house to a pole, following the manufacturer's instructions. Place pole in ground.

BUTTERFLY GETAWAY FLOWER PATTERNS

149

darling dog collars

Be sure your family pet is sittin' pretty wearing one of these dainty cross-stitch collars.

WHAT YOU'LL NEED
Desired-size piece of 14- or 18-count mesh fabric
Cotton embroidery floss as listed in key; needle
Purchased dog collar
Fusible hem tape
⅝- or 1-inch-wide grosgrain ribbon in desired color; thread

HERE'S HOW
1 Tape or zigzag edges of mesh. Find center of chart and of fabric. Begin stitching there. If a longer stitched piece is desired, repeat the pattern, adjusting the size of the mesh and the center point. Use two plies of floss to work cross-stitches over squares of mesh. Work French knots, *page 192,* using two plies of floss.
2 Trim the stitched piece ¼ inch beyond stitching. Fuse under raw edges using hem tape. Cut two ribbons the length of fabric. Use 1-inch-wide ribbon for the pink collar and ⅝-inch-wide ribbon for the green collar. Turn under ends and stitch ribbons alongside design. Place over collar, and fold ribbons to back side. Stitch in place.

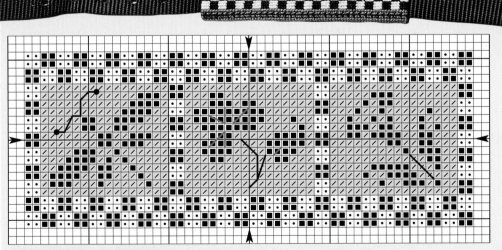

PINK DOG COLLAR PATTERN

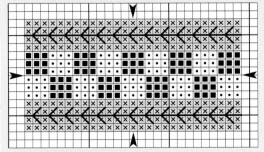

GREEN DOG COLLAR PATTERN

Anchor		DMC	
002	•	000	White
403	■	310	Black
243	✕	988	Forest green
060	◪	3806	Cyclamen
BACKSTITCH			
002	╱	000	White – pink collar (2X)
403	╱	310	Black – both collars (2X)
FRENCH KNOT			
403	●	310	Black – pink collar

Green Collar stitch count:
14 high x 27 wide

Green Collar finished design sizes:
14-count fabric – 1 x 2 inches
16-count fabric – ⅞ x 1⅝ inches
18-count fabric – ¾ x 1½ inches

Pink Collar stitch count:
22 high x 56 wide

Pink Collar finished design sizes:
18-count fabric – 1¼ x 3 inches
14-count fabric – 1½ x 4 inches
16-count fabric – 1⅜ x 3½ inches

151

birdhouse trims

Bring your yard to life with these miniatures hanging from the branches. Re-create these designs on small decorative birdhouses or on larger houses to pamper a chorus of feathered friends.

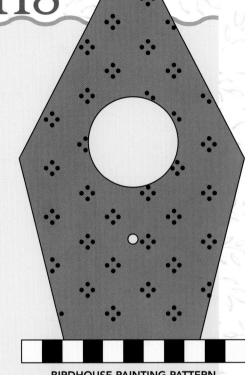

BIRDHOUSE PAINTING PATTERN

WHAT YOU'LL NEED
Fine sandpaper
Tack cloth
Purchased wood birdhouses
Newspapers
White spray primer
Acrylic paints in green, blue,
  tan, cream, red, and black
Medium flat and fine round
  paintbrushes
Toothpick
6-inch piece of ½-inch-diameter
  dowel
Clear gloss spray varnish

HERE'S HOW
1 Lightly sand the birdhouses. Wipe the dust away using a tack cloth.

2 In a well-ventilated area, cover work surface with newspapers. Prime the surface of the birdhouses by spraying with white primer. Let them dry.

3 Paint the roofs green or blue. Paint the main part of the house tan or cream. Paint the top of the base of the birdhouse red. Paint the rim around the edge of the base cream. Let dry. Paint small black checks using a fine brush.

4 Paint tiny dots in clusters of four using a toothpick.

5 To paint flowers, use a dowel. Dip the dowel in red paint, and dot onto surface. Let dry. Add a center dot using the handle of a paintbrush dipped in paint. Paint green leaves using a fine round brush. Paint the perch and the inside of the hole a contrasting color. Let the paint dry.

6 Spray two light coats of clear gloss varnish, allowing to dry between coats.

BLUE BIRDHOUSE ROOF PAINTING PATTERN

This delightful wagon is just the right size to hold feed for neighborhood critters. The pattern pieces are so easy to cut, that you'll want to make more to use as planters and storage bins.

totin' wagon

WHAT YOU'LL NEED
Tracing paper and pencil
½-inch-thick piece of pine
Tilt-blade table saw; jigsaw
Sandpaper; 18-inch-long piece
    of ¾-inch-square wood
Drill and ¼-inch drill bit
1-inch-long finishing nails
Hammer
1⅝-inch-long piece of
    ¼-inch-diameter dowel
Tack cloth; nail putty
White spray primer
Medium flat and fine liner
    paintbrush
Acrylic paints in yellow, red,
    aqua blue, green, white, and
    pale orange
4 pegs for wheels
6-inch-long piece of
    ½-inch-diameter dowel
Clear gloss spray varnish

HERE'S HOW
1 Enlarge and trace the patterns, *pages 156–157*, onto ½-inch pine. Cut out all pieces. Use a tilt-blade table saw to cut the angles on the front, back, and bottom pieces. Sand edges until smooth.

2 To make the handle, use ¾-inch square pieces of wood. Cut a 14-inch-long handle. Cut two 2-inch-long pieces. Glue a 2-inch-long piece to each side of the 14-inch length, each about 2 inches from the end to create the handle.

3 Drill a ¼-inch hole in the center of each wood wheel piece as indicated on the pattern. Drill holes for handle and tongue as indicated.

4 Attach each side to the base of the wagon. Nail two or three 1-inch finishing nails into the bottom edge to attach to the base. Attach each end side, nailing at top and bottom.

5 For the tongue, refer to the diagram and drill a hole to accommodate a ¼-inch-thick dowel. Cut a 1⅝-inches-long piece of dowel. Insert the dowel into one end of tongue, push through drilled handle, and glue in place on each end. Do not glue onto the handle piece.

6 Attach tongue piece and handle to the bottom of the wagon. Refer to the pattern for placement. Nail together with three finishing nails.

7 Fill in nail spots with putty. Sand smooth. Wipe dust off with a tack cloth.

8 Spray entire wagon with primer. Let dry. Paint entire inside of wagon yellow. Let dry.

9 Draw a 1-inch border around edge of sides with a pencil. Paint outer border red. Paint inside aqua blue. Paint wheel edges blue and front and back surfaces green. Paint star shape red. On inside surface of wagon, dip the handle of a paintbrush into red paint and dot surface. Paint wheel pegs yellow. To make red flowers, dip a ½-inch dowel into red paint and dot onto surface. Let dry. Add yellow dots in flower centers. Use a fine liner brush to paint stems and leaves. Add small white dots between flowers. Paint red and orange checks along handle. Paint handle bars green and blue.

10 Spray wagon with varnish. Let dry. Assemble wheels when dry.

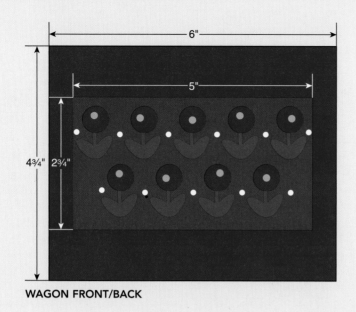

WAGON FRONT/BACK

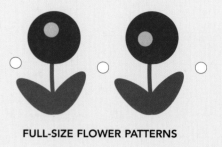

FULL-SIZE FLOWER PATTERNS

WAGON SIDE VIEW

WAGON HANDLE ATTACHMENT (TONGUE)

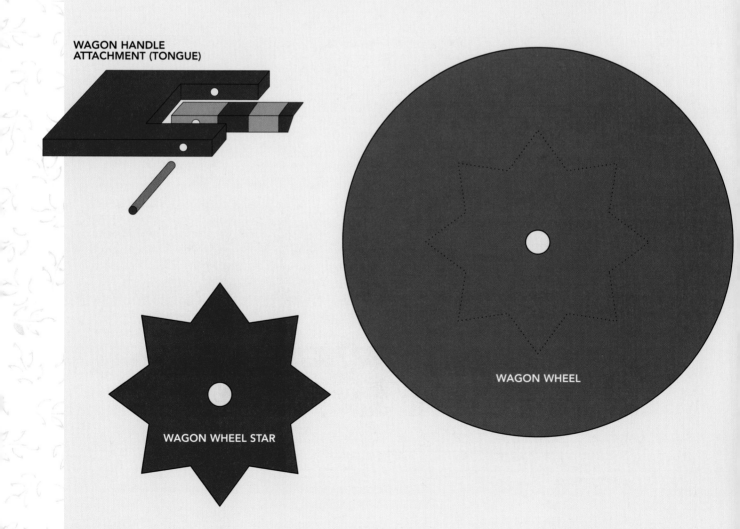

WAGON WHEEL STAR

WAGON WHEEL

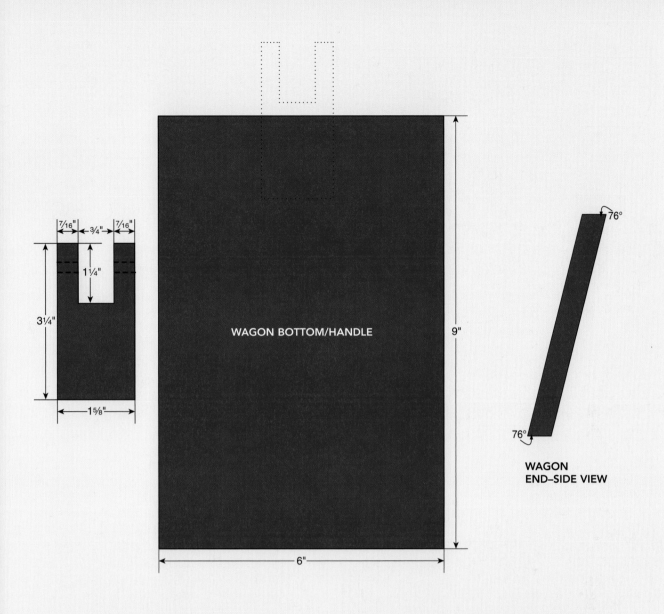

7/16"   3/4"   7/16"

1¼"

3¼"

1⅝"

WAGON BOTTOM/HANDLE

9"

6"

76°

76°

**WAGON
END–SIDE VIEW**

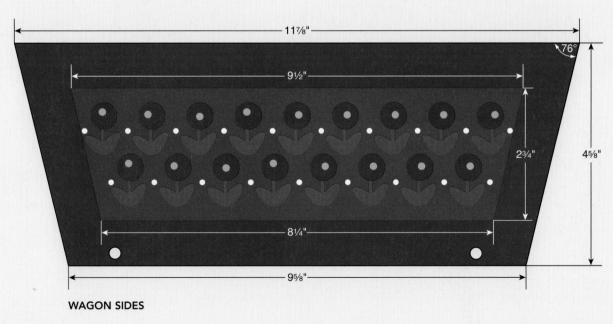

11⅞"

9½"

76°

2¾"

4⅝"

8¼"

9⅝"

WAGON SIDES

TOTIN' WAGON

splish-splash birdbath

A flea market table forms an interesting base for this one-of-a-kind birdbath which provides hours of entertainment.

WHAT YOU'LL NEED
Small, round wood table (available at flea markets, discount stores, or thrift shops, approximately 24 inches high and 14 inches in diameter)
Sandpaper; tack cloth
Round, white plastic serving tray approximately 16 inches
Exterior construction adhesive
White spray primer
Tracing paper; pencil
Acrylic paints in bright gold, red, black, olive green, white, and blue
Flat and round paintbrushes
Clear exterior spray sealer

HERE'S HOW
1 Sand the surfaces of the table. Wipe dust with a tack cloth.

2 Center and glue the tray atop the table. Let dry.

3 In a well-ventilated work area, set the bird bath upside down. Spray a light coat of primer on the table and the back of the tray. Let dry. Apply a second light coat. Let dry. Turn the birdbath right side up.

4 Trace the star pattern, *below,* onto tracing paper, and cut out. Trace the pattern onto the sides of the tray as shown in the photograph, *opposite,* leaving space between stars. Paint the background behind the stars blue. Let dry. Paint a yellow-and-red checked border around the tray edge. Let it dry.

5 Using the photograph as a guide, paint the base of the birdbath with base colors and let dry. Paint flowers, checks, stripes, and dots where appropriate for the shape of the table. *To paint dots,* dip the handle of a paintbrush or a round pencil eraser into paint and dot onto the surface. *To paint flowers* referring to the pattern *below,* first paint the center by making a dot with a pencil eraser dipped into paint. Use a small round brush to add the petals and leaves. *To make checks or stripes,* use a flat paintbrush. Let the paint dry. *To make two different shades of paint,* such as the reds on the base, add a few drops of black to darken the color. To lighten a color, add white.

6 Place the birdbath upside down in a well-ventilated work area again. Spray with an exterior sealer. Let dry.

BIRDBATH FLOWER GUIDE

BIRDBATH STAR PATTERN

gazebo bird feeder

Painted with primary colors, this towering feeder is a popular gathering place for busy backyard birds.

WHAT YOU'LL NEED

Tracing paper; pencil; scissors
¾-inch-thick pine for base
¼-inch-thick pine for all scallops
Four 1×1-inch pine pieces, each
   10¼ inches long
Table saw and a scroll saw,
   jigsaw, or band saw
Sandpaper; ½ inch brads
6×6-inch copper-topped deck
   post cap
White spray primer
Medium flat and small
   paintbrushes
Small, purchased birdhouse
Acrylic paints in blue, red,
   orange, green, yellow, and
   white; tape
Broad-tip black permanent
   marker
Small scrap of crafting foam
Thick, white crafts glue
Pencil for stamper

6-inch-long piece of ⅝-inch dowel
1⅛-inch finishing nails
Ruler; wood glue
Adhesive, such as Liquid Nails

HERE'S HOW

1 Trace the full-size patterns, *pages 164–165*, onto tracing paper, cut out, and trace onto wood. Use ¾-inch-thick pine for the base and ¼-inch-thick pine for all of the scalloped areas. Cut four 1×1-inch pieces of pine, each 10¼ inches long. These will be the posts to hold the roof. Use patterns to cut out remaining pieces. Sand the surfaces until smooth.

2 Assemble the four outer scallops for base. Notice there are two different sizes, indicated by the dotted lines. Cut two of each. Place the same sizes opposite each other. Nail three ½-inch brads into each corner. Nail all corners together. Assemble each piece together so that all four sides measure equally and will be square.

3 Assemble the inner scalloped square in the same manner. Place the four 1×1-inch posts in each corner, and nail into the corners.

4 Nail the top side scallops onto edge of roof with at least one brad in each corner.

5 Prime all surfaces, including the copper-topped deck post cap, with a white spray primer. Let primer dry.

6 Paint all blue areas as shown in the photograph, *opposite*. Paint the roofs red and the trim green. Paint the roof scallops yellow. Let dry. Add red dots by dipping the handle of a small paintbrush in red paint. Dot onto surface. Let dry. Using the red scallop roof patterns, *page 165*, transfer the roof designs onto the red painted roofs by cutting out the patterns. Beginning on the bottom, center the pattern on each roof and tape down. Draw around the scalloped edge. Move the pattern up to draw the next row of scallops, staggering the position as shown, *above*.

continued on page 162

7 After you draw scallops in pencil, shade each scallop with orange paint. Use a small flat brush and very little orange paint. The brush should be nearly dry. Brush along one side and the bottom of each scallop, creating lighter highlights. Paint as consistently as possible. Let dry.

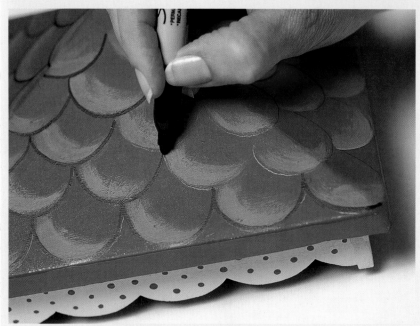

9 To make stars on the post, first make a stamping tool. Trace the star pattern, *page 164*, onto a scrap piece of crafting foam. Cut out the shape and glue it onto the flat end of a pencil. Dip the stamper into white paint and stamp onto surface. You may need to touch up stars with a fine brush. Practice a few on paper first. Add small white dots using the handle of a paintbrush.

8 Use a broad-tip permanent marker to draw the black scalloped lines on both roofs.

10 To paint yellow flowers as on *page 164*, use a ⅝-inch-thick dowel, cut to about 6 inches long. Dip one end into yellow paint, and dot onto surface. Center one flower in each scallop. Let dry. Add flower center using the handle of a large brush dipped in red paint. Paint small green oval leaves. Let dry.

11 When all surfaces are painted, finish assembling the pieces. Measure to find center of green square, and position scallops and posts. Nail from the bottom with at least one 1⅛-inch finishing nail in each corner.

12 Position the outer scallop to fit symmetrically onto the square. Nail from the bottom of the green base with 1⅛-inch finishing nails. Secure with two nails in each corner.

13 Use wood glue on top of post to adhere the roof piece. Position roof over wood post with posts fitting snugly inside of end cap.

14 For small birdhouse base, cut a piece of ¼-inch wood the same size as base. Cut a 1×1-inch square out of the center of the wood piece. This will create a hollow area to fill with glue. Using the photograph on *page 160* as a guide, paint the surfaces and let dry. Glue to the bottom of the small birdhouse. Let dry. Use a generous amount of adhesive in the hollowed-out area to affix to the painted roof on top of the bird feeder.

15 Spray with a clear gloss varnish. Let dry. Apply a second coat, if needed. Let dry. Be cautious to spray very light coats onto the roof area so marker does not run.

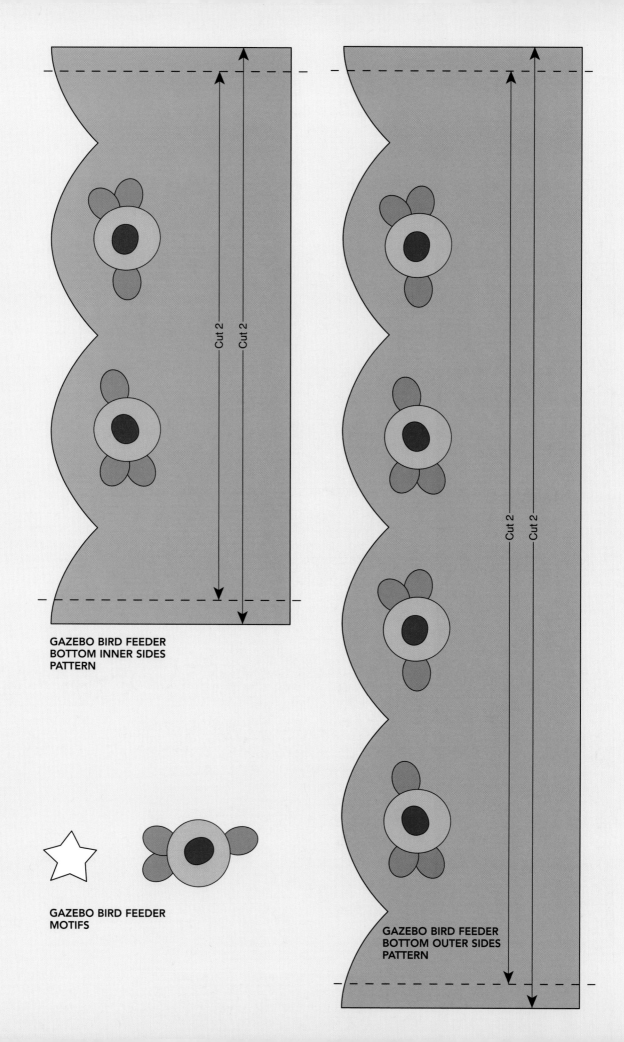

Cut 2

Cut 2

**GAZEBO BIRD FEEDER
BOTTOM INNER SIDES
PATTERN**

**GAZEBO BIRD FEEDER
MOTIFS**

Cut 2

Cut 2

**GAZEBO BIRD FEEDER
BOTTOM OUTER SIDES
PATTERN**

164

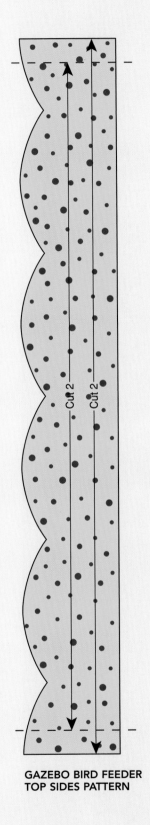

GAZEBO BIRD FEEDER
TOP SIDES PATTERN

Cut 2

Cut 2

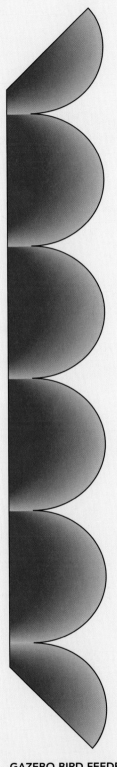

GAZEBO BIRD FEEDER
LARGE ROOF
SCALLOP PAINTING
PATTERN

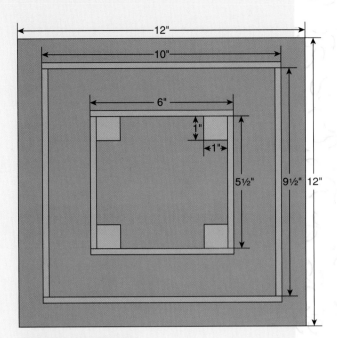

GAZEBO BIRD FEEDER
BOTTOM SCHEMATIC

12"

10"

6"

1"

1"

5½"

9½" 12"

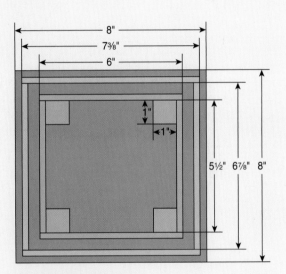

GAZEBO BIRD FEEDER
TOP SCHEMATIC

8"

7⅜"

6"

1"

1"

5½" 6⅞" 8"

GAZEBO BIRD FEEDER
SMALL ROOF
SCALLOP PAINTING
PATTERN

outdoor entertaining

arties are always fun to plan, especially when outdoor entertaining is on the menu. Mary's illustrations will inspire you with wonderful ways to make your next get-together one that will be remembered for years to come.

old-fashioned waterer

Pick a fresh bouquet from the garden to display in this charming watering can, embellished with crackles of paint and colored-pencil designs.

WHAT YOU'LL NEED
Watering can
White spray primer
Acrylic paint in dark red and
  yellow ocher
1-inch flat paintbrush
Crackle medium
Tracing paper; scissors
Colored pencils in red, green,
  and blue
Antiquing gel
Disposable foam brush
Rag
Clear satin spray varnish

3 Paint at least two heavy coats of crackle medium, allowing to dry between coats.

HERE'S HOW

1 Spray the watering can with white spray primer. Let it dry.

2 Paint the outside of the can dark red. Let it dry. Paint a second coat. Let dry.

HOW DO YOUR CANDLES GLOW?

4 Brush a smooth coat of yellow ocher paint over the entire surface. Apply generously and evenly in one direction, while keeping the brush moving. Let the yellow paint dry and crackle.

continued on page 170

old-fashioned waterer — *continued*

5 Trace the full-size heart pattern, *opposite*, onto tracing paper. On wrong side of tracing paper, use red, green, and blue colored pencils to retrace the lines as shown, *above*.

7 Use colored pencils to color in the design as shown, *above*. The coloring does not have to be heavy, just even and neat. Some of the paint will show through the pencil color. Color the raised areas of the can, if desired.

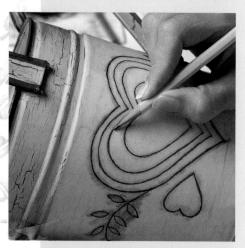

6 Place traced design, colored-pencil side down, onto watering can. Retrace the pencil lines to transfer the colored pencil design onto the can.

8 Use a foam brush to spread antiquing gel over the entire surface of the can.

9 Using a rag, gently rub off the antiquing gel, leaving the gel in the cracks.

10 Spray the entire can with several light coats of clear satin varnish. Allow to dry between coats. It is important to spray the first two coats on very lightly so the pencil color does not run.

170

**OLD-FASHIONED WATERER
HEART PATTERN**

171

sparkling pots

Add pizzazz to any party by filling these painted terra-cotta flowerpots with illuminating sparklers.

WHAT YOU'LL NEED

Clay flowerpots in desired sizes
Outdoor acrylic paints in yellow, red, robin-egg blue, dark blue, white, pink, green, and black
Medium flat and fine liner paintbrushes
Tracing paper and pencil
Black permanent marker
Duct tape
Colored aquarium gravel
Sparklers

HERE'S HOW

1 Begin with clean dry pots. Paint the base colors with a medium flat paintbrush. Paint the bottom portion of pot, then the rim and the inside. You can use the color combinations pictured, or make up your own. Let dry.

2 Add details to each pot. To paint flowers, trace the patterns, *below*, onto tracing paper. Color the back of the tracing paper with a soft lead pencil. Tape the pattern onto the pot in position and draw over the tracing lines with a sharp pencil to transfer pattern onto base of painted pot. Add details with a fine liner brush.

3 To make the small blue dots or the white flowers, dip the handle of a paintbrush into paint, and dot onto the pots. Paint the lines with a fine liner brush.

4 Outline the flowers on the blue pot with a permanent marking pen.

5 Tape the bottom hole shut with a piece of tape on the inside. Fill the pot with aquarium gravel in a contrasting color. Insert sparklers into gravel.

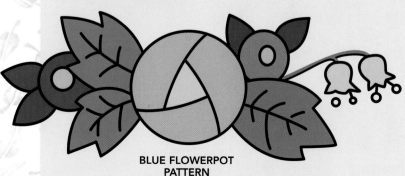

BLUE FLOWERPOT PATTERN

ORANGE FLOWERPOT PATTERN

RED FLOWERPOT PATTERN

beehive centerpiece

Your guests will buzz about this imaginative beehive that graces the tabletop.

WHAT YOU'LL NEED

Foam egg, such as Styrofoam, at least 5 inches high
Sharp knife; aluminum foil
Nonstick spray cooking oil; twine
Decoupage medium; bowl
Straight pins
Small, sharp scissors
Yellow acrylic paint; paintbrush
Bakeable clay, such as Sculpey, in pink, green, blue, red, yellow, and white
Dull knife; baking dish
Thick white crafts glue

HERE'S HOW

1 Using a sharp knife, cut the narrow end off the foam egg, cutting as straight as possible.

2 Wrap a piece of foil snugly around the wide end of the egg, smoothing out the bumps and wrinkles.

3 Spray a light coat of nonstick spray cooking oil over the foil.

4 Pour approximately ¼ cup of decoupage medium into a bowl. Dip twine into the bowl, soaking it with decoupage medium. Pin one end of the twine at the base of the foil-wrapped egg. Wind twine tightly around the egg from the bottom up until the egg is completely covered. Add more decoupage medium as needed. Cut the twine and pin the end in place.

5 Let the twine dry on the foam dome until it is set enough to remove from the foil without distorting the shape. Remove the straight pins before removing the twine. Before it is completely dry, cut a tiny entrance with a small pair of sharp scissors. Then let the beehive dry until hard.

6 Paint the beehive with yellow acrylic paint. Let dry.

7 To make the pink clay flowers, form a bell-shape piece. Add a yellow ball to the center, and press gently together. To make blue flowers, form small grape-size blue balls and gently flatten them. Press smaller yellow balls into centers. To make the white daisy, form a round red ball and gently flatten it. Form six pea-size white balls around the center and press into it. To make the yellow tulip, first form a round ball and flatten it on one end. Take a dull knife and press a V shape into the flat side. Place the knife crosswise and make another V shape.

8 To make leaves, form a round ball, flatten it, and pinch one end to form a point. Make a crease down the center of the leaf with a knife blade held at an angle. Bake the pieces on a baking dish according to the manufacturer's instructions. Let cool.

9 Glue the flowers and leaves in place using crafts glue. Let dry.

party-time place cards

Make guests feel regal at your next get-together with these personalized pastel place cards.

WHAT YOU'LL NEED
for each place card
3¼×3½-inch piece of heavy white paper
2¾×1¼-inch piece of pink paper
Lightweight white and yellow paper for bee
Lightweight white paper for dragonfly
Black and red paper for ladybug
Scissors; ruler
Tracing paper; pencil
Fine-tip black marker
Colored pencils in bright green, light blue, purple, yellow, and white
Glue stick

HERE'S HOW
1 Fold the piece of heavy white paper in half with the 3¼-inch edges together. Use the bright green pencil and a ruler to make marks along the edges every ¼ inch for the place card front. Color in each corner and every other square with the bright green pencil.

2 Outline the pink rectangle with black marker. Glue to the center of the place card.

3 Trace the desired patterns, *below*, onto tracing paper. Trace the patterns onto appropriate pieces of white or colored paper. Cut out pieces using small, sharp scissors. Glue the bee body to the wings, the dragonfly body to the wings, or the ladybug wings to the body.

4 Use the marking pen to add the line details as shown on the patterns. Use colored pencils to add color as indicated on the patterns.

5 Glue bugs onto the place cards as shown, *opposite*. Use the marking pen to add the antennae details and the guest's name.

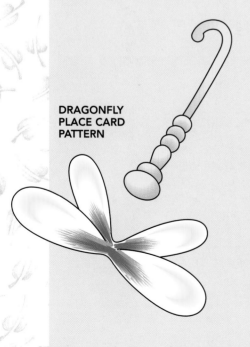

DRAGONFLY PLACE CARD PATTERN

LADY BUG PLACE CARD PATTERN

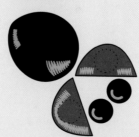

BUMBLEBEE PLACE CARD PATTERN

nature's best topiary

Capture some of Mother Nature's brightest creations with a towering topiary that includes fruits, flowers, and fluttering butterflies.

WHAT YOU'LL NEED

Scissors
20 wide, wood craft sticks
Hot-glue gun and hot-glue sticks
7×6-inch wood box, such as a
  compact disc holder
Construction adhesive
Four 1½-inch-diameter wood
  knobs
White spray primer
Newspapers
Serrated knife
Foam balls, such as Styrofoam,
  in 5, 6, and 8 inches
32-inch piece of ½-inch dowel
Paper clips
Foam blocks, such as Styrofoam
Putty knife
Hand-applied textured ceiling
  plaster (not a spray type)
Sea sponge
Acrylic paints in olive, brown,
  and white
Bakeable clay, such as Sculpey,
  in pink, yellow, green, red,
  white, orange, purple,
  and blue
Black crafting wire
Darning needle
2 artificial butterflies
  on wires
Yellow shredded paper

HERE'S HOW

1 Use scissors to cut off the rounded ends of the craft sticks. Arrange five sticks vertically on one side of the wood box. Glue in place using hot-glue gun. Repeat on each side of the box. Let dry.

continued on page 180

179

2 Use construction adhesive to glue a wood knob in each corner of the box bottom. Let dry. In a well-ventilated and covered work area, spray box with white primer. Let dry.

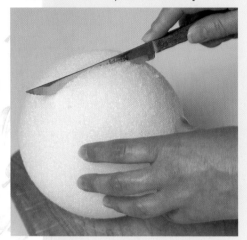

3 On a protected surface, cut each of the foam balls in half using a serrated knife.

4 On the flat side of each foam ball half, cut a V-notch down the center. Remove the cut pieces of foam.

5 Place one half of the small foam ball on one end of the dowel with the end of the dowel in the center of the ball. Glue to dowel. Add the other half and glue in place. Repeat with the other two foam balls, placing each about 5 inches below the previous one.

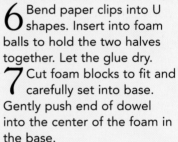

6 Bend paper clips into U shapes. Insert into foam balls to hold the two halves together. Let the glue dry.

7 Cut foam blocks to fit and carefully set into base. Gently push end of dowel into the center of the foam in the base.

8 Spray-paint the foam balls and the dowel with a light coat of primer. Let dry.

9 Use a putty knife to apply textured ceiling plaster to each of the foam balls, pressing into the crevices between the foam ball halves. Let the plaster dry until firm. Use a sea sponge to paint the textured balls olive. Let dry. Paint the topiary stem using a combination of brown and white. Let dry.

10 Shape the flowers from clay. *To make the top pink flowers,* shape clay balls slightly smaller than golf balls. Flatten slightly. Shape a rounded triangle center from yellow clay. Apply to center of pink ball. Use a drinking glass to add rounded lines as shown on *page 178.* Add green leaves as desired. Make approximately 12 flowers.

11 *For cherries,* roll nickel-size circles from red clay. For stems, cut 2½-inch single stems or 5-inch double-stems from wire. Press the wire ends into tops of cherries. Shape and add green leaves at top of stem. Make approximately 18 single or pairs of cherries.

12 *For bottom flowers,* roll and flatten golf-ball-size balls from desired colors of clay. Add marble-size centers. Make approximately 24 flowers. Bake clay in oven according to the manufacturer's instructions.

13 Glue flowers in place, using the photograph, *page 178,* as a guide. Let dry.

14 To add butterflies, use a needle to poke two holes in foam balls. Insert wires into holes. Fill top of base with yellow shredded paper.

flower-border basket

Easy-to-make felt flowers are a fresh breath of spring on any woven basket.

WHAT YOU'LL NEED
Tracing paper
Pencil
Scissors
Felt in lavender, pink, red,
  yellow, white, blue, and dark
  and light green
Needle
Matching threads
Small pom-poms in yellow
  and red
Hot-glue gun and hot-glue
  sticks
Basket

HERE'S HOW

1 Trace the full-size patterns and enlarge the circle pattern, *pages 184–185*, onto tracing paper, cut out, and trace onto felt pieces. Cut out shapes.

2 *To make the lavender or white daisy,* bring the ends of each petal to the center, overlapping each other, and sew several stitches by hand with a needle and thread in matching color to hold in place. Sew a yellow pom-pom in the center.

3 *To make the round flower,* use a sewing needle and matching thread to sew a loose stitch approximately ¼ inch from the edge around the circle. Pull and gather the thread as you go. When you have sewn all the way around, it should have gathered into a smaller circle. Sew several stitches in the center to hold it in place. Sew a pom-pom in the center.

4 *To make the blue flower,* sew a pom-pom in the center.

5 *To make the leaves,* use green thread and a needle to sew a line of stitches down the center, beginning at the tip and sewing to the base of the leaf. Pull the thread slightly to gather the leaf into a gentle curl shape.

6 Glue the flowers to the edge of a basket using a hot-glue gun. Let cool.

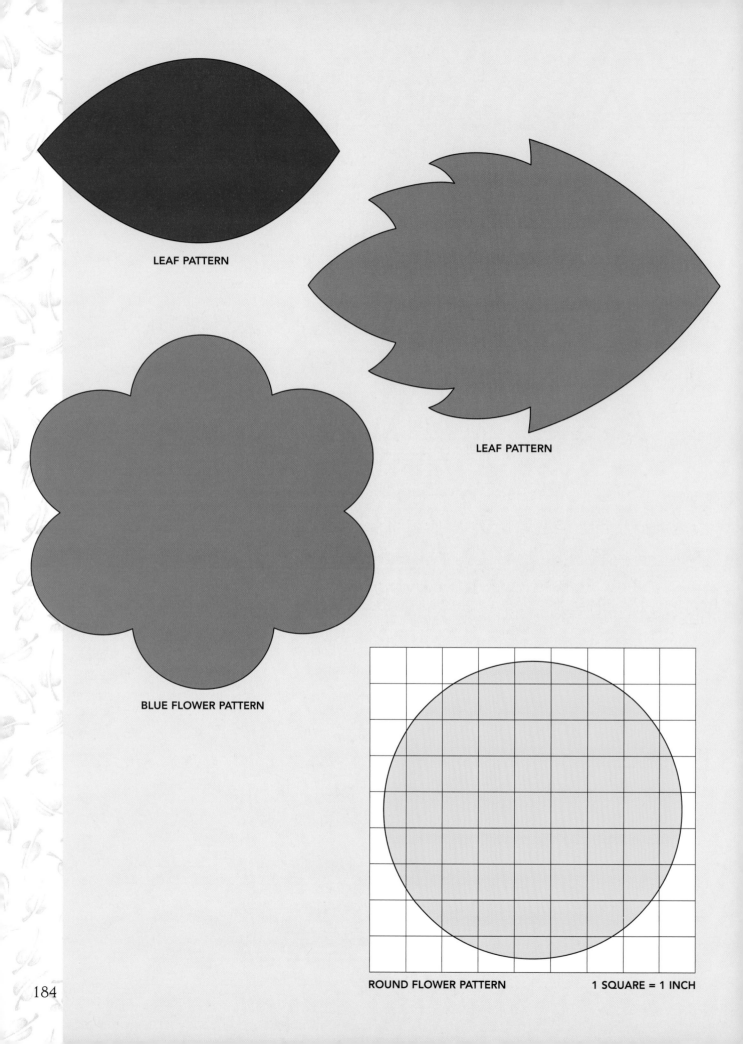

LEAF PATTERN

LEAF PATTERN

BLUE FLOWER PATTERN

ROUND FLOWER PATTERN   1 SQUARE = 1 INCH

DAISY FLOWER PATTERN

185

summertime linens

No matter what the weather, you'll feel like the sun is shining with these delicate linens gracing the table.

WHAT YOU'LL NEED

30×30-inch piece of 28-count cream Lugana fabric for tablecloth

18×18-inch piece of 32-count cream Lugana fabric for each napkin

Cotton embroidery floss, as listed in keys; needle

Two 3-yard packages of 7mm pink silk ribbon for embroidery (Bucilla #566) for tablecloth

One 3-yard package of 4mm yellow silk ribbon (Bucilla #666) for napkin

HERE'S HOW

1 Tape or zigzag the edges of the fabric to prevent fraying. *For napkin*, measure 4 inches from each edge on one corner. Mark this as the center, and begin stitching the center of the chart there. *For tablecloth*, measure 5 inches from each edge on a corner. Mark this as the center and begin stitching the center of the chart there. Repeat for each corner of the tablecloth, rotating the design as you work each corner. Use two plies of embroidery floss to work all cross-stitches over two threads of fabric. Work the backstitches and straight stitches according to the key.

2 To finish tablecloth, trim square 2¼ inches past the design. Pull one thread on each of the four sides, 1 inch past the design. Weave pink ribbon through the rows with the pulled threads, alternating under and over two threads at a time.

3 Finish the napkin in the same manner as the tablecloth, except trim the fabric 1¾ inches past the design. Pull thread 1 inch past the design and weave in the yellow ribbon.

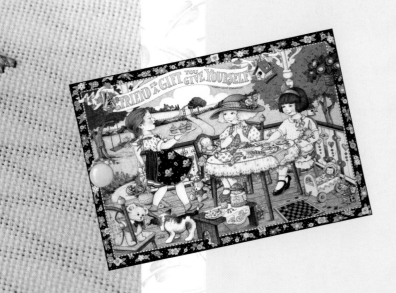

SUMMER BOUQUET TABLECLOTH PATTERN

Anchor	DMC	
002	000	White
1025	347	Salmon
877	502	Medium blue-green
266	581	Moss green
057	601	Dark cranberry
063	602	Medium cranberry
062	603	True cranberry
075	604	Light cranberry
326	720	Bittersweet
303	742	Tangerine
024	776	Pink
140	813	Powder blue
255	907	Parrot green
297	973	Canary
875	3813	Light blue-green
386	3823	Yellow
031	3833	Raspberry
410	3843	Electric blue
324	3853	Autumn gold

BACKSTITCH

683	500	Deep blue-green – leaf veins (2X)
1041	844	Beaver gray – all other stitches (2X)
410	3843	Electric blue – daisy (2X)

STRAIGHT STITCH

002	000	White – flower highlights (2X)

Stitch count: *63 high x 69 wide*
Finished design sizes:
28-count fabric – 4½ x 5 inches
32-count fabric – 4 x 4⅜ inches
36-count fabric – 3½ x 3⅞ inches

SUMMER BOUQUET NAPKIN PATTERN

Anchor		DMC	
002	•	000	White
1025	♥	347	Salmon
877	▢	502	Medium blue-green
266	✕	581	Moss green
063	▽	602	Medium cranberry
062	+	603	True cranberry
075	=	604	Light cranberry
303	◇	742	Tangerine
132	●	797	Royal blue
140	☆	813	Powder blue
255	○	907	Parrot green
297	∧	973	Canary
087	✶	3607	Fuchsia
060	‖	3689	Mauve
875	╱	3813	Light blue-green
410	◉	3843	Electric blue
324	▦	3853	Autumn gold

BACKSTITCH

683	╱	500	Deep blue-green – leaf veins (2X)
877	╱	502	Medium blue-green – stem (3X)
1041	╱	844	Beaver gray – all other stitches (2X)
410	╱	3843	Electric blue – daisy (2X)

Stitch count: *52 high x 49 wide*
Finished design sizes:
32-count fabric – 3¼ x 3 inches
28-count fabric – 3¾ x 3½ inches
36-count fabric – 2⅞ x 2¾ inches

index

PAGE 174

191

thanks

from the bottom of my heart...

...to these people who shared their talents

Craft Designers

SUSAN M. BANKER
20–21, 56–57, 80, 90, 138, 140–141, 158, 177, 178

DONNA AND GAYLEN CHESNUT
20–21, 106–107, 124–125, 155–156, 160

BARBARA SESTOK
72, 150, 186–187

MARGARET SINDELAR
12, 18, 26–27, 34–35, 46, 50–51, 54–55, 62–63, 66–67, 84–85

ALICE WETZEL
10–11, 17, 22–23, 30–31, 38, 42–43, 58–59, 78, 82, 94–95, 96–97, 100–101, 103, 106–107, 110–111, 116–117, 118, 120–121, 124–125, 130, 134–135, 146, 152, 154–155, 159, 168–169, 172–173, 174, 182

Model

Chester the dog

Photographers

Andy Lyons, Scott Little

Photostyling

Carol Dahlstrom
Donna Chesnut, Assistant

Product Sources

CROSS-STITCH FABRIC
Zweigart
262 Old New Brunswick Road
Piscataway, NJ 08854
908/271-1949

EMBROIDERY FLOSS
Anchor
Consumer Service Department
P.O. Box 27067
Greenville, SC 29616

DMC
Port Kearney Building 10
South Kearney, NJ 07032-0650

RIBBON
CM Offray & Son Inc.
Route 24, Box 601
Chester, NJ 07930-0601
908/879-4700

SEWING MACHINE
Viking #1 Plus
Husqvarna Viking Sewing
  Machines
31000 Viking Parkway
Westlake, OH 44145
440/808-6550

WOOL FELT
National Non Wovens
www.nationalnonwovens.com
sales@nationalnonwovens.com

Stitch Diagrams

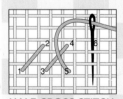
HALF CROSS-STITCH

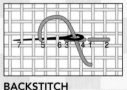
BACKSTITCH

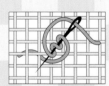
FRENCH KNOT

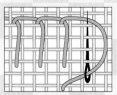
BLANKET STITCH

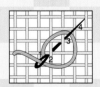
LAZY DAISY

RUNNING STITCH

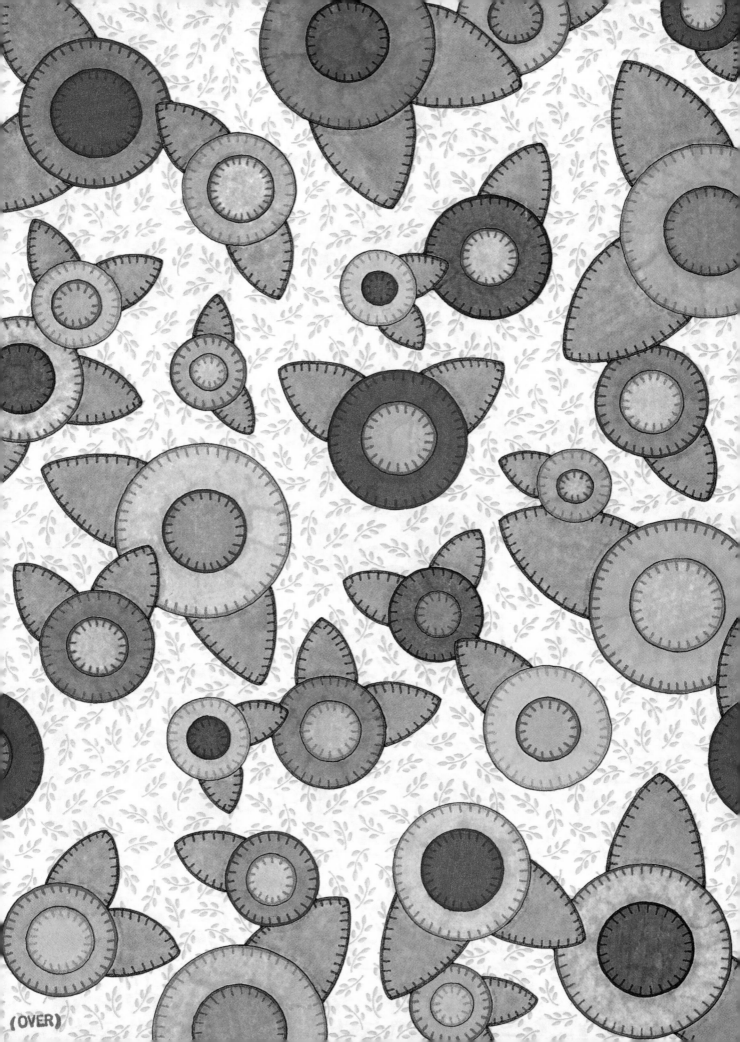